The Invisible Men of Adoption

Gary Coles

MERMERUS BOOKS
AUSTRALIA   2010

The author can be contacted via
BookPOD
PO Box 6015
Vermont South
VIC 3133
Australia
email: sales@bookpod.com.au

Copyright © Gary Coles 2010

This book is copyright

Apart from any fair dealing for the purposes of private study, research, criticism or review, as permitted under the Copyright Act, no part of this book may be reproduced by any process without written permission.

First published in 2010

ISBN: 978-0-646-54848-7

Dedication

To Evelyn –
for encouraging me to delve and to write about what I found

Foundations

"You are the bows from which your children as living arrows are sent forth.

The archer sees the mark upon the path of the infinite, and He bends you with His might that His arrows may go swift and far.

Let your bending in the Archer's hand be for gladness;

For even as He loves the arrow that flies, so He loves also the bow that is stable."

From *The Prophet*, by Kahlil Gibran

"Grief fills the room up of my absent child."
William Shakespeare

Credo

"Do not go where the path may lead,
Go instead where there is no path and leave a trail."
                                               Ralph Waldo Emerson

CONTENTS

Introduction   1

Solo
1. The Adoption Sandwich   6
2. Birth father citings   15
3. And father makes three   32
4. Finding the father within   44
5. The fortunate minority   57

Duo
6. Birth parents who remain mum   72
7. Guilt throwers and guilt catchers   79
8. The role of control   83
9. The incentive to search   92
10. Personal effects   116

Trio
11. Introducing a fresh perspective   122
12. The long and wounding road   124
13. Love's labour's lost   172
14. The enlightened family   186
15. To command the boundless sea   196

References   208

The Invisible Men of Adoption

Introduction

"One ship drives east and another drives west
With the selfsame winds that blow.
'Tis the set of sails
And not the gales
Which tells us the way to go."

Ella Wheeler Wilcox

In 2007, I had an idea for a book about a neglected topic. I believed that the time had come for the birth father to be recognised as a man who has a significant contribution to make to post-adoption matters. Other projects intervened, but ***The Invisible Men of Adoption*** refused to disappear, because, I realised, there was much to reveal. In particular, I saw that birth fathers were under-represented in stories, articles and books about adoption reunions. In 2009, the unveiling began.

Whilst what I have written is for all those people whose lives have been changed by adoption, my specific interest is the men who were separated from their children by this social practice.

The Invisible Men of Adoption is about the impact of adoption on birth fathers and the influence of birth fathers on adoption. I expect that what I say will resonate with women who have lost children through adoption. Also, I anticipate that my input into the discussion about adoption issues will help all, men and women alike, whether they be birth parents, adoptive parents, adopted persons, members of families touched by adoption, or those working in the fields of adoption placements and post-adoption services, to understand the viewpoint of the birth father. My intentions are dual – to inform and to challenge commonly held views.

The Invisible Men of Adoption

Because I am a birth father, I believe that I am well placed to draw on my experience and thus share what I have learned. My research has embraced the adoption experiences of other birth fathers, as well as family members who have reached out to birth fathers. Currently, I am the manager of a post-adoption services organisation and in this role I oversee the provision of support to all members of the adoption community.

I have written two previous books about adoption, ***Ever After: Fathers and the Impact of Adoption*** and ***Transparent: Seeing Through the Legacy of Adoption***. Whilst these works pay attention to birth fathers, they also address more general adoption matters. ***The Invisible Men of Adoption*** draws upon my earlier publications, but centres on the men who fathered children who were raised by other, adoptive, parents. However, I do not consider birth fathers in isolation. I acknowledge that the father is but one member of the family of origin, the others being the birth mother and their child. Ultimately, I highlight the importance of post-adoption interactions among the three family members, as adults, facilitated by tolerance and generosity.

I have chosen ***The Invisible Men of Adoption*** as the title, because the vast majority of birth fathers remain unseen. I base my claim upon their habitual absences at conferences, support group meetings and seminars and their low numbers in enquiry statistics. Ideally, more birth fathers should be seen and heard. With this desired state in mind, discovery is at the core of this book, in the multiple senses of 'disclosing information about', 'learning about' and 'unearthing' birth fathers. Fundamentally, the title is both a statement of fact and a challenge aimed at birth fathers.

The Invisible Men of Adoption is a call to those birth fathers who have not admitted that losing a child to adoption has had an impact on their lives to own up to their pain and to acknowledge the consequences their actions have had for others, notably the birth mother and their child. For some birth fathers, these may be undertakings they had not contemplated previously. There are other birth fathers who know the grief of separation, but

The Invisible Men of Adoption

are unable to make progress beyond this basic recognition. ***The Invisible Men of Adoption*** is also reminder to others that they not only encourage birth fathers to emerge from the shadows, but also welcome their emergence.

The book is divided into three sections. The first, ***Solo***, sets the adoption scene and then illuminates the impact of adoption on birth fathers. Drawing on the scant material written by and about birth fathers, I reveal how birth fathers feel about the loss of their child. ***Duo*** is a bridging section. Adopted persons, birth mothers and birth fathers are the expanded focus. As a precursor to the final section, there are chapters devoted to the action impediments of secrecy, denial, guilt and locus of control. ***Duo*** goes on to discuss not only the factors that either impede or encourage birth fathers and adopted persons from seeking one another, as adults, but also the personal benefits that accrue from the exploration. I encourage all adopted persons to search for their birth fathers. Birth fathers and adopted persons who do not acknowledge their connectedness are living incomplete lives because they are denying their consanguinity and the impact of the one on the other. On this basis, I advocate that birth fathers become more venturesome in outreach activities. The final section, ***Trio***, addresses the wounds caused by the separation of the members of the family of origin and their desirable participation, as three willing individuals, in the healing process.

Beyond encouraging birth fathers to take responsibility for the legacy of their actions upon themselves and others, ***The Invisible Men of Adoption*** promotes and demonstrates the benefits of birth fathers being included as a primary participant in interpersonal matters, such as the mending of emotional wounds, which were caused by the initial separation of the three members of the family of origin, and reunions. This key role for the birth father <u>in a tripartite setting</u> has not been addressed by anyone else in adoption literature.

The naming of the parties involved in adoption is often a contentious issue. I have chosen to use the terms 'birth parents' and 'adoptive parents' throughout my book, except where a quoted source uses another term, *eg* 'biological father', or 'natural mother'. Birth and adoptive parents are the most commonly used terms in the literature and, as such, have the advantage of being understood, universally. Some authors eliminate the space after 'birth', preferring 'birthmother', etc. I concede that it can be argued, because birth fathers were not always present at the birth (it is mandatory for birth mothers), that it is impertinent that they be accorded this adjective. However, the pedantic alternative of 'conceiving' father, is, to me, akin to the term 'biological'. Both suggest artificial laboratory settings and an utter lack of emotional involvement, which, based on the available data, is seldom so. For the child who is adopted and grows to adulthood, I have adhered to convention and used 'adopted person'. Overseas usage favours 'adoptee', but to me, this term seems impersonal.

I trust that, for those of you who have unravelled your adoption experience, my book is a reinforcement of the actions you undertook and an acknowledgment of the results you have achieved. I hope that, for those people who have deferred an exploration of the influence of adoption on their lives (especially birth fathers), my book provides the catalyst for you to begin your journey of self-discovery and integration. Based on my experience, the journey is absolutely worthwhile.

Through my exposure of the 'invisible men', I hope that not only the other members of the family of origin but also the broader community, including the helping professions gain a better appreciation of what it means to be a birth father. My ultimate ambition is that the birth father stereotype be overturned – that these men are the beneficiaries of a social transformation from marginalisation to inclusion.

The Invisible Men of Adoption

Solo

CHAPTER 1

The Adoption Sandwich

"It has been said that to find inner peace and self we must leave home and risk travelling into the wilderness ... In adoption it is the reverse: we must leave the wilderness or the abyss and take the risk of finding home and our true selves."
— quoted in **issues**, the newsletter of the Canterbury Adoption Awareness and Education Trust (Number 21, Oct–Dec 2001)

Adoption has existed for millennia. From Greek mythology we know of Oedipus, abandoned by his father because the Oracle of Delphi had prophesied that Oedipus would commit patricide. He was rescued and raised by King Polybus and Queen Merope as their own. They did not inform him that he was not their natural son and so, when he fled to avoid the fate the Oracle had predicted for him, he believed that he was protecting himself from committing murder. In his wanderings, when confronted by a threatening stranger, Oedipus killed him. Of course, he had unknowingly killed his father. Oedipus married the widow of the man he had killed, thus fulfilling the second and better known part of the prophecy – that he would marry his mother.

Then there is Moses, hidden in the bullrushes, adopted by the Pharaoh's daughter and ultimately reunited with his birth mother. His is the story that encapsulates the idealised outcome of an adopted person growing up to be good and strong, blessed by the love of two mothers. Note that the father is absent.

In each of these cases, three participating entities were involved – birth parents, an adopted person and adoptive parents.

The Invisible Men of Adoption

Public figures who know the legacy of adoption include adopted persons such as operatic diva Kiri Te Kanawa, comedian Judith Lucy, Olympic diving gold medallist Greg Louganis, singer Deborah Harry, author Patsy Adam-Smith, playwright Edward Albee (*Who's Afraid of Virginia Woolf?*), Henry Morton Stanley (he of "Dr Livingstone, I presume" fame), several Roman emperors and serial killer Son of Sam, as well as birth mothers Louise Hay, Charmian Clift and Pauline Collins and adoptive parents Brian Wilson, Ronald Reagan, Joan Crawford, Diane Keaton, Nicole Kidman, Madonna and Rosie O'Donnell. Oscar winner Frances McDormand is both an adopted person and an adoptive parent. Among famous music entertainers, there is at least one acknowledged birth father – David Crosby of The Byrds and then Crosby, Stills, Nash & Young. Albert Einstein fathered a daughter, "who was discreetly put up for adoption" (Bryson, 2003, p108). Apart from his longevity as an entertainer, George Burns (1896–1996) achieved another milestone. At his death bed, six weeks after he celebrated his 100th birthday, was George's 73 year-old adopted son. Adoption has also featured in the movies. In Howard Hawk's *Red River* (1948), set on a cattle drive along the Chisholm Trail, a centrepiece is the conflict between Tom Dunson (John Wayne) and his adopted son Matthew Garth (Montgomery Clift). The adoption of disturbed Billy in *A Soldier's Daughter Never Cries* is the catalyst for the disintegration of an adoptive family. Among the more recent movies with adoption at their core are *Secrets and Lies*, a gritty story of search and reunion and *Juno*, a Hollywood fantasy, which portrays a teenage pregnancy and the subsequent relinquishment of the baby as events that leave the wisecracking, eponymous heroine utterly unaffected. *Mother and Child*, released in 2010, has a fine portrayal by Annette Bening of a birth mother's trauma, within a setting that manages to convey the impact of adoption on members of the family of origin, as well as the prospective adoptive parents.

It is estimated that in my home state of Victoria, Australia, one in five people is touched by adoption. That is approximately one million Victorians, involved directly, or as a ripple effect, through the families of the birth and the adoptive parents, the spouse or partner of the adopted person and their families and children. Clearly adoption has influenced a significant proportion of the population. Other Australian states and New Zealand report similar figures.

Many of the studies about adoption refer to the Adoption Triangle (or Triad). In using this terminology, authors such as Sorosky, Baran and Pannor (1978), Lifton (1979), Tugendhat (1992) and Verrier (1993) are referring to the triumvirate of birth parents, adoptive parents and the child. Sorosky *et al* (*ibid*) and Tugendhat (*ibid*) titled their books *The Adoption Triangle* and this is a common and well-understood term, not only in the literature, but also at adoption conferences. Griffith (1991) takes this linkage a step further, by noting that, in the Adoption Triad model, "The three major parties to the adoption – the adopted person, the adoptive parents and the birth parents ... have equal rights and responsibilities" (Section 2, p10).

The Adoption Triangle can be viewed as the means for uniting the key participants in a perceived shared benefit and common dependencies: "Removal of children from young single mothers for married couples was seen as a 'perfect solution' for all three parties:
- the mother could hide the fact that she'd transgressed and 'been caught,'
- the adoptive parents could hide the fact of their infertility and pretend the child was 'as if born to' them,
- the adopted child could hide his/her 'immoral parentage' and pretend to be 'as if born to' the adopters.

Adoption therefore became an institution founded on triple shame, and dependent upon secrecy and lies" (Pace, 2005).

The triangle suggests an equilateral relationship, which may be ideal, but does not always reflect reality. O'Shaughnessy (1994) expresses a concern about the restrictiveness of the traditional model: "Triangularization removes a range of institutions and actors (including social workers) from the primary picture of adoption, encouraging the misrecognition of adoption as a consensual transaction between, and in the interests of, the members of the triangle" (p21).

In a later paper, Griffith (1998, p21) muses how the evolution of the adoptive relationship mirrors the opening up of adoption. He notes the evolution from closed adoption (dyad), in which the birth parents were disposed of by an adoption order, through the Adoption Triangle period, notable for the searches undertaken for each other by adopted persons and birth mothers, to, ultimately, the Adoption Circle, highlighted by reunions of adopted persons with both their birth parents, as well as siblings, grandparents and other relatives.

Two decades earlier, Lifton (1979) had used the term Adoption Circle in another context. Speaking of the USA and referring to the traditional Adoption Triangle, she wrote: "But actually there are many more people involved – the social workers who place the child, the lawyers and the doctors who arrange private adoptions, the judges who seal the records and the clerks who guard the records ... I see the game as a circle. The Adoption Circle. Sometimes the baby is in the centre of the circle and the other players are outside. ... the game can also be played with the baby outside the circle and everyone else within" (pp13–14 of the 1988 edition of *Lost and Found*). The 'game' Lifton refers to here is the pretence that the adopted person belongs to the family raising her, that she never had any other parents. Rod Holm (2000, p338), in speaking of his experiences as an adoptive father and post-adoption counsellor, also refers to the 'adoption circle', to embrace the participation of others beyond the traditional triad.

Yet, no matter in which context the terms Triangle or Circle are used, they imply a neat symmetry, a balance, with no loose ends. Patently, this is not true in practice. Adoption is a complex network of relationships, some linear, many indirect. Both traditional models refer to the adoptive parents and the birth parents as entities. In the case of adoptive parents, this is usually so, as the parents act together to adopt and raise the child. The birth parents act independently; otherwise, in most instances, the adoption would not have occurred.

The Invisible Men of Adoption

There is an implicit assumption, particularly in the Adoption Triangle, that it is the birth mother alone who experiences the loss of her child, sometimes as the result of a decision that has been forced upon her because of a lack of support from the birth father. This focus on the birth mother makes the assumption that the birth father does not matter; he is not affected by the loss of his child, he does not have feelings, nor perhaps does he deserve to have them. Typically, adoption and post-adoption are seen as mother–child issues.

Adoption does not begin and end with the handing over of a child to 'new' parents. In the social situation prior to the 1970s, a period when illegitimacy was typically stigmatised, the adoption option became the primary solution the moment the child's conception was confirmed. Parents, social workers and sometimes, the church played key roles in convincing the birth mother of the rightness of her 'choice'. Adoption was not a last minute decision made at birth; the seeds had been sown nine months earlier. (In fact, the literature is loaded with personal narratives of birth mothers, who, once they had given birth and held their baby, had tried desperately to rescind the decision to adopt. They were too late.) In such an unforgiving social environment, often the adoption was linked to the conception of the child. The man who, when the child was born, became the birth father was certainly there for the initiating event. And, once a father, always a father – there is no such figure as a former father.

The reference to birth parents in the literature is often actually about a sole parent, the birth mother, and so does not reflect the reality of conception, leading the casual reader to assume that adopted persons were conceived immaculately without sperm. Despite this common, misconceived portrayal, there are good reasons why birth mothers have received more attention than birth fathers. The overwhelming majority of adoption studies about parenting issues, particularly personal narratives, are by birth mothers. Since Shawyer (1979) broke ground with *Death By Adoption*, many other birth mothers have emerged to demand that their voice be heard and their concerns addressed. In a snowball effect, funding for further studies has resulted, as well as the establishment of support groups. A greater understanding of issues affecting birth mothers, by birth mothers, the adoption community and the general public, has been the result.

Men have not been as forthcoming. The typical male reticence to express feelings and vulnerabilities means that a man is less likely to admit to a loss caused by adoption. Adoption is seen as women's business, a sentiment echoed by the ratio of the genders attending adoption conferences. At the 7th Australian Adoption Conference held in Hobart in May 2000, only 15 of the 171 attendees were male; women outnumbered men by a factor of 10 to 1. This imbalance between male and female is also apparent at support group meetings for adopted persons, although the degree is not as marked as for birth parents' meetings, where any birth father is conspicuous by his presence.

Birth fathers are not represented adequately in the traditional adoption models, particularly the Adoption Triangle, where they are regarded, if at all, as an appendage. To address this deficiency, I propose a fresh model, the Adoption Sandwich (see Figure 1 below).

The Sandwich acknowledges the role the birth father plays in conception, as well as recognising that birth mother and birth father have unresolved issues, certainly with their child, but, frequently, also between themselves. The model also notes the stronger bond between mother and child. Stiffler (1992, p19) points out that whereas mothers and their child are linked in at least three ways: biologically during pregnancy, psychologically and genetically, fathers can claim only the latter two connections. The different dynamics operating between adopted persons and their birth and their adoptive parents, as well as any internal conflicts this causes an adopted person, are also highlighted. In this model, applicable to closed adoptions (by which I mean adoptions arranged around birth and adoptive parents who were strangers and remain so unless brought together by the adopted

The Invisible Men of Adoption

person as an adult), the adopted person is truly the meat in the sandwich, for they occupy the position at the nexus between the birth and adopted families. At another level this central positioning is appropriate – the ideal that adoption represents a focus on the interests of the child is often touted.

For the sake of visual clarity, the remaining influencers are not shown. Other family members affected by adoption, including the parents of the birth mother and the birth father, as well as of the adoptive parents, full and half siblings of the adopted person and the spouses of the birth father and the birth mother, not forgetting extended family, could be represented by extra fillings in the sandwich. They are the tomato, the lettuce, the beetroot, the alfalfa, the cucumber and the mayonnaise of a high stack sandwich, not neat, but with bits hanging out. The social workers, post-adoption counsellors, legislators and academics involved with adoption could be the wrapping around the sandwich. They are assisting, observing, making changes to the framework. The plate on which the sandwich sits could represent the social climate of the moment.

Other family members outside the conventional core have been seldom recognised in adoption literature. Stiffler (1992) is one of the few to have summarised the impact of adoption on extended family. She writes: "A grandmother may originally have wanted to raise the baby herself, but was given no voice in the matter. If a grandfather was the one who urged his daughter or son to surrender an infant for adoption, there may be lingering grievances, regret and guilt ... Some grandparents, who were never informed of the pregnancy in the first place, are not aware of the existence of the child until a reunion takes place. They have a choice to be coldly cautious, or to become catalysts in the process of family integration and reconciliation" (p28).

Sibling rivalry is a fact of human existence, a means by which children of any age vie for their parents' attention. Stiffler (1992) notes: "A sibling raised by his birth parents has one set of birth parents, while a reunited adopted person has the attention of two or more. If birth parents are married to other spouses, there are additional stepparents and half siblings who come into the picture. Envy or grief may arise if one family has provided more material or educational advantages, and the cultural gap is broad" (p29).

The Adoption *Sandwich

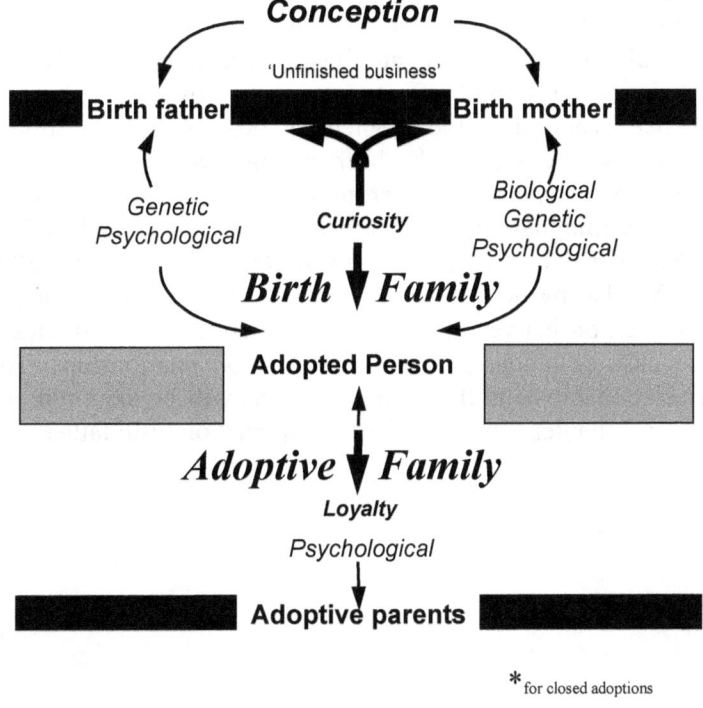

*for closed adoptions

Figure 1

Spouses too, are affected by adoption. For example, the spouse of an adopted person and/or either of the birth parents may feel threatened by the approach of an adopted person who seeks reunion. A husband or wife of a person with an adoption experience may fear a divided loyalty, being no longer the centre of attention and affection. This reaction may, in turn, affect the response of the person with whom the reunion is sought. Members of extended families can and do have an impact on the dynamics of adoption and so cannot be ignored.

These then are the key players in the adoption game. The relative dominance of the principal players has changed as adoption practices have evolved and the impact of the various members of the 'support cast' has waxed or waned, according to the social climate. Curiosity and loyalty, depicted on the Adoption Sandwich as push-pull effects, represent powerful behavioural influences, centred on the adopted person. The relative strengths of curiosity, focused on the birth parents, versus loyalty to the adoptive parents, can have a profound influence on some adopted persons' willingness to search for their origins, as noted by Lifton (1988), Griffith (1991), Brodzinsky *et al* (1993) and Coles (2002).

Whilst, by definition, adoptive parents are not participants in the reunion between birth parent and child, their attitudes can either ease or hinder pre- and post-reunion relationships. These interrelationships and their manifestations will be explored in the following chapters, in particular their impact on birth fathers.

CHAPTER 2

Birth father citings

"To lose one parent, Mr Worthing, may be regarded as a misfortune; to lose both looks like carelessness. Who was your father?" – The Importance of Being Earnest, by Oscar Wilde

This chapter addresses how birth fathers are seen by others, as well as the way they perceive themselves.

Fathering and mothering

'To mother a child' does not have the same connotations as 'to father a child'. The use of 'mother' as a verb conveys caring, cherishing, nurturing and possibly, when taken to extremes, overprotection and pampering. 'To father', however, means being the source or originator of a child, 'the sower of the seed'. The traditional use of the verb 'father' does not encompass the maternal qualities of kindliness and affection. Fathers are more likely to be seen as protectors and providers, providing a secure environment in which children can be conceived and raised. Mothering is acknowledged as a way of caring, of meeting a child's physical and emotional needs, before and after birth. To father a child is to reproduce progeny through a woman. The act of fathering may be a single ejaculation; it is a brief event. Mothering is visible and, of necessity, a durable role. It should come as no surprise then that one birth mother, having lost her child, uttered "adoption is so unnatural" (Inglis, 1984, p71).

The Invisible Men of Adoption

Historically, this dichotomy between mother and father has had a profound impact on the status of mothers and children. Prior to the late twentieth century social acceptance of single parenthood, a child's legality was vested in the father. Of paramount importance, both socially and legally, was the mother's relationship to the father. Marriage was the legitimate link that forged a child's social parentage.

In circumstances where a child was considered to be illegitimate, "This generally meant the child was the child of the mother only, and the usual obligations of a father to that child could be evaded on the basis of the mother's relationship to him" (Inglis, 1984, p1). Inglis goes on: "She is a legal parent by demonstration of her fecundity. His biological fatherhood is both in marriage and out of it less easily demonstrable. Fatherhood is a more socially derived state than motherhood, at least in defining who is actually a parent" (p7). She continues: "This unfortunate nexus between parents, stemming from their lack of a marital tie, perhaps drove many men, who may have been able and willing to provide emotional support through a pregnancy and relinquishment, to simply evaporate" (p7). Thus, there are valid social and biological reasons why birth mothers and birth fathers may have reacted differently to the news of the pregnancy and to the decisions required to be made about the future of their child.

The perspective of the socially constructed unfettered male reinforces the stereotypical view of birth fathers as men who have shunned their responsibility for paternity. However, there is mounting evidence that many birth fathers do not fit this rigid model, that other factors have influenced their behaviour.

Birth father views

Prior to the 1970s, adoption was seen as a contract between the relinquished child and the grateful adoptive parents, brokered by a social worker and/or adoption agencies. Birth mothers had no rights to the child they had readily 'let go', in the interests of

The Invisible Men of Adoption

'putting the event behind them' and 'getting on with the rest of their lives'. It was assumed, in this social climate, that birth mothers, consumed by the shame of producing an illegitimate child, wished to remain anonymous and eschew any thought of a possible future reunion.

It was not until the late 1970s that the actual voice of the birth mother began to emerge. Sorosky *et al* (1978) and Shawyer (1979) challenged the hitherto entrenched belief that mothers wanted to forget their relinquished children. As birth mothers found the courage to come forward and their stories began to be heard, it became obvious that they had never forgotten their relinquished children, had suffered unresolved grief as a result of their loss, were not intent on maintaining anonymity and would in fact welcome contact. Authors such as Inglis (1984), Harkness (1991), Schaefer (1991), Collins (1992) and Robinson (2003) have published graphic, inside-out accounts about the birth mother experience. These personal narratives have been reinforced by studies undertaken by Winkler and van Keppel (1984) and Bouchier, Lambert and Triseliotis (1991).

The paucity of literature on birth fathers is reflected in comments made about their status. Mary Martin Mason (1997) notes that "research about birth fathers continues to be as scarce as are their faces at adoption conferences" (p15). Evidence in support of this assertion is available from at least one source. In each instance, the registrants for the 7th, 8th and 9th Australian Adoption Conferences, held in 2000, 2004 and 2008, included but one birth father. Whilst birth mothers have found attendance at support groups to be an integral part of their healing process, few men have been motivated to make the same discovery.

Marshall and McDonald (2001, p98) point out the imbalance between the volume of enquiries made by birth mothers and birth fathers of the Post Adoption Resource Centre in Sydney, New South Wales. Of 5945 queries made by birth parents between 1991 and 1998, but 456 (7.7%) came from birth fathers. Of 157 mediations made to adopted persons on behalf of birth parents during the same period, only six (4%) were initiated by birth fathers. Isabel Andrews (personal communication, 2008) reported that only 1–2% of Adoption Jigsaw's search initiating clients are birth fathers. Approximately 85% of searches are initiated by adopted persons, approximately 9% by birth mothers and the remainder are siblings, aunts, separated children (*ie* foster- and step-) etc. Even taking into account that many birth fathers are unaware of their status (which is explored in the next segment of this chapter), these are significant imbalances.

Mason, noting that birth fathers are often known as 'the shadowy figures of adoption', used this phrase to generate the title of her 1995 book, which she based on interviews with birth fathers in Minnesota, USA. She called her publication *Out of the Shadows*. (Curiously, Mason uses the term 'birth father' to denote all fathers separated from their children. Only twelve of the seventeen men she interviewed had lost children through adoption, including nine when the child was an infant.)

Wells (1994) is another who refers to the birth father as the peripheral figure: "When we think of the parent of a child for adoption, we think of the mother. When we think of the grief experienced through that loss, we think of the mother. Even the term 'birth parent' suggests the mother ... birth fathers are a mere shadow. They don't exist ... They were barely mentioned" (p67).

Continuing on this theme of the mystic male, Lifton (1994) commented: "He is the more abstract concept, but the adoptee's (*sic*) anger toward him may be as deep or deeper than toward the mother. He is, after all, a double abandoner: he abandoned the mother as well as the child. Yet there is an attraction to this missing father; his absence puts him in the romantic tradition of the loner, just passing through and disappearing on his way to the next frontier" (p192). He is an evanescent figure. Note here that when Lifton speaks of the scope of abandonment she is referring only to how a birth father is perceived, not how he views the consequences of his actions.

Clapton (2003) refers to several examples in the literature of conflation, where the terms 'birth parent' and 'birth mother' are used interchangeably. This careless switching between the

The Invisible Men of Adoption

descriptors implies that the experiences of the birth father, himself a birth parent, are both unimportant and identical to that of the birth mother (pp41–43). Clapton also takes issue with the stereotypical view of fatherhood, that of fathering being action orientated, embracing activities fathers share with their children, in other words what fathers 'do' (2003, pp47–54). As he points out, this outdated and narrow view ignores the fatherhood of birth fathers, men who have no social contact with their child during his or her upbringing.

It is plain, that as a grouping, birth fathers have been little studied and are poorly understood. Clapton comments that "there is little acknowledgment of their fatherhood in any sense" (*The Age*, 19 August 2000). Society is seen as playing a crucial role in the suppression of the birth father voice, *eg* "Fewer still are encouraged to acknowledge their loss in a society that believes they feel nothing" (Mason, 1997, p16) and "My experience is that men go through feelings in relation to guilt similar to those of natural mothers, but it isn't socially acceptable for men to come forward" (Tugendhat, 1992, p23).

As noted by one writer, "adoption is a woman's world" (Severson, undated, p7). This view is reinforced by a birth father's personal plea for recognition, *viz*, "I get tired of the way pressure groups and the media always refer to birth mothers. I've been very emotional about my daughter and I want people to know that fathers have feelings too" (Tugendhat, 1992, p32).

An example of legislation – from Victoria, Australia

To put society's view of birth fathers into context, it is important to note that historically birth fathers' names often did not appear on the birth certificate. This is not proof that these birth fathers were neglectful. Rather, the absence of the father's name on the record does support the notion that many birth fathers may have been completely unaware of the pregnancy and of the birth of their child. This explains in part the low numbers of birth fathers of that era who come forward. They cannot acknowledge a paternity they never knew was theirs to claim.

Nicholls and Levy (1992) undertook research to determine the role of birth fathers in cases involving the relinquishment of children, after the introduction of the *Adoption Act* in Victoria in 1984. Under this Act, introduced to supersede previous Acts and their amendments, birth fathers were accorded equal rights and legal status, with the proviso that they had been named by the birth mother and had their paternity established. This involved a complicated process, not only to prove paternity, but also to include the father in the decision-making to determine the future for the child. In Nicholls and Levy's study (p63), only 26 of the 54 birth mothers named the father of their baby. The most common reasons birth mothers gave for not naming the birth father were the father not being advised of the pregnancy (so contact was not wanted), the birth father's reluctance to be involved in pre-adoption counselling or decision-making and the birth mother's wish not to have the father, who knew of the pregnancy, to be involved in the decision-making. Nicholls and Levy concluded that, because only in a minority of cases had birth fathers been named and subsequently involved in relinquishment counselling and then usually when there was a significant relationship between the birth parents, the amended legislation had not achieved its aim to increase the involvement of birth fathers in planning for the future of their children.

A similar study by Nankervis (1991) reached parallel conclusions about the effect of the *Adoption Act 1984*. To quote:

> "... it can be concluded that while there have been important gains in giving legal consent for involved fathers since the implementation of the Act, there has been little improvement in the overall nature and the rate of involving natural fathers and the majority are still excluded from the decision making (*sic*) process regarding their child.
> The research clearly indicates that a major factor working to exclude fathers is the <u>reluctance by a majority of mothers to identify the natural father</u> ...

The Invisible Men of Adoption

> Furthermore the findings indicate that the father's involvement is significantly associated with the closeness of the parent's relationship, both at conception and during the relinquishment phase. The critical point mediating involvement appears to be the mother's acknowledgment of some current contact with the father during the decision making time" (p1) [emphasis in the original].

Nankervis also noted "... that since the new legislation, social workers do not refer to the father, nor advocate his rights any more frequently than previously" (p3).

The key messages arising from both pieces of Victorian based research are:

- Legislation did not force entrenched attitudes to be changed,
- To a significant extent, whether or not a birth father is involved in deciding the future of his child depends on the mother's attitude towards him, and
- The quality of the relationship between the birth parents is critical to the involvement of the birth father.

Birth fatherhood

Have birth fathers brought this neglect and non-involvement upon themselves? In 1989, Sorosky *et al* reported the results of interviewing sixty adoptive parents about their attitudes towards their children's birth parents: "Most of the adoptive parents indicated that they had an understanding, accepting, and sympathetic attitude toward the birth mother. In marked contrast to this, only a small number had positive feelings toward the birth father, with an overwhelming number expressing varying degrees of negative or indifferent feelings" (p79).

The stereotypical view of the birth father is as the cad who has abandoned the birth mother; the man as the villain, the woman as the victim. In 1992 Tugendhat commented "Men can

The Invisible Men of Adoption

get away with denying paternity and often do" (p25). This sentiment is echoed in *Living Mistakes*, by Kate Inglis (1984). One birth mother interviewed by Inglis claimed: "... plenty of women have cause to hate the fathers of their children before they are born – and long after" (p141). Other women who contributed to this anthology had this to say about fathers who abandoned them: "Men are so bloody slippery and this was my first encounter with real trouble with a man. I hadn't thought of that, I'd assumed he'd believe me" (p25), "He just got away with it" (p36), "He didn't want to marry me. He was terrified of what he'd landed in" (p104) and "He was a bit of a bastard really ... He just withdrew when there was nothing left in it for him" (p104).

According to Severson (undated), "To many in the adoption world, the birth father truly has been the Magic Man with an incredible disappearing act" (p3). Severson then asks: "Do birth fathers deserve this sorry reputation?" and responds, "To some degree they do. Some guys have run because they wanted to. They've abandoned their child and the mother of their child with full knowledge of exactly what they were doing. And they did it anyway" (p3). However, Severson does not consider this view to be representative of birth fathers as a whole. He goes on: "But some guys – far more, I think, than anyone believes – ran, not because they wanted to, but because they didn't know what else they could do. They didn't know how to translate *I want to do the right thing* into some plan of action. They didn't know what *doing the right thing* meant" (p3) [emphasis in the reference].

Ross is a birth father who fits into the last category (Wells, 1994). Speaking about learning of birth mother Fern's pregnancy, he says: "We'd been together about a year at that stage and I was very committed to her and intended marrying her later on ... But when she became pregnant, I had no idea what to do or where to start" and "I didn't know what to do – so all I could do was to continue to support her and write to her all the time. I felt helpless" (p68). Witney (2003, p12) puts the bewilderment of the birth father into perspective, noting that, based on her study of a significant number of birth fathers, they were "as shocked and confused as their partners." Schaefer (1991, p230) notes that for many birth fathers, not doing what was 'right' can be correlated with immaturity.

The men's state of bafflement, on occasions, numbness, was sometimes taken advantage of by social workers, predominantly women, intent on putting, within the family of origin, the interests of the child first and perhaps the birth mother second. Typically, there was scant regard for and little attempt made to understand the underlying male reaction to the imminent relinquishment of the child. Some social workers considered that the interests of the adoptive parents exceeded those of any member of the family of origin, pushing the birth father even further from consideration. Sorosky *et al* (1989) commented: "A negative attitude has long persisted among adoption agencies about involving birth fathers. The result has been that adoptive parents have had little information about birth fathers to pass on to their adopted children" (p79). This, Sorosky *et al* conclude, has produced a legacy: "Since information about the birth father is not usually provided to the adoptive parents ... , his child can develop only one of two images of him: (a) the feeling that there is something wrong with him and that he is the villain who shunned all responsibility and victimized the birth mother; or (b) no image at all, as if the child has only one birth parent" (p49).

Another factor which frustrates birth fathers' intentions to do the right thing is, as Clapton points out the intervention role of parents, who were seen in many cases (almost 50% in his study of thirty men) as having been the main influence to have the child adopted (2003, p90). These sentiments are echoed by a birth father in Cicchini's (1993) research: "I was confused, ambivalent, wanted to have my son, but fearful of losing my parents' approval, sad, powerless, guilty and in pain" (p8). Cicchini's West Australian study involved thirty birth fathers who, in response to a media campaign, volunteered to participate. More than two-thirds of the respondents had little or no say in the decision to relinquish their child, acknowledging that the child's mother and/or her parents were the ones who organised the adoption. Birth father Kevin (PARC, 1998) tells of relinquishing his daughter, not because he and her birth mother were impoverished or unable to care for the child, but "simply because of the shame and disgrace this would bring to our families, especially mine" (p19). He and the birth mother rued the decision – "We were very weak and stupid. What we did was soon to be realised to be a serious mistake which would affect both our lives dramatically forever" (*ibid*). Schaefer (1991, p230) reports the findings of a reunion registry service in the United States: "[These birth fathers] were surprised themselves at their lasting feelings of guilt after their children were given up. They confided ... their guilt at allowing themselves to be manipulated by their parents ..." These men also confided their guilt at being too immature to make sound decisions about the future of their child. Pannor, in Gediman and Brown (1991), observes that birth fathers' non-involvement in adoption decisions has created an image of them being "uncaring, uninterested and irresponsible", which is "unfair and inaccurate" (p274).

Severson's assertion that the stereotype of the birth father disappearing in a cloud of rapidly retreating dust does not stand up to close analysis, a conclusion that is supported by data from other sources. For example, Lifton (1988) identifies four categories of birth father. The first she calls the Macho Father. He is the man who denies paternity. This is the disgraced birth father, the one who has his sport and moves on. The remaining categories fall outside this stereotype and display varying degrees of concern for the child. Of The Father Who Cares, Lifton (1988) has this to say: "Far from being a 'swinger', or the older man who seduced the young girl, he was usually the same age and social level – sometimes he was the boy next door. His dependency on his own family often made it difficult for him to accept responsibility. He may have been advised by his parents to deny paternity, rather than risk a large financial settlement" (p158). The Missing Father's disappearance does not always represent a lack of concern for his child. Men may be deeply wounded by the experience and retreat within their pained selves. The Ambivalent Father may deny at first he has fathered a child, later admit responsibility, but then behave erratically, preferring to forget 'it' ever happened.

Clapton (2003) reports that in nearly all cases, the men in his study had been going steady with the birth mother. As he points out, this "goes very much against the stereotype of young mothers whose babies are adopted after a brief association with the father" (p68). Most of the couples were teenagers who had been careless. Harkness (1991), quoting from earlier work by Iwanek, notes: "Research further shows that in the fifties and sixties studies of pregnant single women repeatedly found that the father was someone they had been involved with for long periods, some ranging from a few months to a few years" (p22). Further, Nicholls and Levy (1992) note that the relationship between birth mother and birth father at the time of the conception of the child was boyfriend-girlfriend for 37 out of 54 cases. 'Casual social relation' applied in only ten situations (p63).

Passmore and Coles (2008, p2) found a correlation that supports the above findings. Of the 27 birth fathers in their study, twenty were in a steady dating relationship with the birth mother at the time their child was conceived, one was engaged and two were in a de facto relationship.

Reactions to the loss

Early studies about the impact of adoption focused on the adopted person and the birth mother. There was a tacit assumption that the father did not suffer any after effects; that any concerns he might have about the conception, pregnancy and birth evaporated before or with the adoption of his child. This conclusion was in part conditioned by the view that birth fathers were 'not there', so how could they possibly have an emotional response? There were some who convicted birth fathers outright – they did not deserve to have feelings, period. As for the men themselves, who, at the time the adoption took place, had not appreciated the long term consequences of losing a son or daughter, many were alarmed to find that years after the adoption they were still suffering, but reluctant to release their pain to scrutiny by themselves or the public. For some men, it was a relief to find that they were not alone; other birth fathers who participated in the studies published in the past two decades reported similar experiences. From these landmark late twentieth century and early twenty-first century investigations, two themes stand out. In general, birth fathers **do** care about the children they fathered and the legacy of adoption is a permanent scar for birth fathers.

Expressions of guilt and shame surface when birth fathers speak of not being there for their child. As Steve articulated for the camera (Woolmington, 1992): "I felt guilty about how I'd treated his mother and him, letting him go." One of the thirty birth fathers in Cicchini's (1993) pioneering study stated bluntly: "I am guilty of not being responsible" (p12). Ross, the birth father who tells his story in Wells' (1994) collection of narratives, reflects "I wasn't there – and I still feel guilty about that ... I think I felt mainly guilty about not being there to support Fern. All I could do was write – about three times a week" (p68). There is a pervasive sense of loss of their child, as expressed by Nick in Tugendhat (1992): "He had never forgotten his daughter. She was always there in the back of his mind" (p32) and in Cicchini (1993): "I have always felt there is something missing from my life – a void, and a wondering if she has been well cared for" (p10). Brown (2002) reports a multi-facetted reaction: "I felt awfully guilty for abandoning my pregnant girlfriend and a great deal of pain at losing my son" (p8). He goes on to describe the consequences in the following terms: "... a shameful compartmentalized secret ... anguish ... fear and guilt ... confusion ... gave way to depression ... I felt powerless" (*ibid*). Brown concludes: "I never got over such a major life event" (*ibid*).

A key finding of Clapton's 1996–2000 study was "that these men cared and still do, some more deeply than others, but all seriously and durably" (*The Age*, 19 August 2000) and "birth fathers can feel as haunted by the child's absence as birth mothers do" (*ibid*). Schaefer's account of her personal loss and the search for her son acknowledges the feelings of the birth father: "He knew more than anyone what this meant to me, because it meant the same thing to him. His loss was as deep as mine" (1991, p272).

Of the predominantly mature-aged men in Cicchini's study, 67% indicated that they thought about their relinquished child frequently; another 13% said that the child was in their thoughts constantly. Almost three-quarters (74%) of the men reported that the loss of their child was a moderately upsetting (or worse) experience. The majority of the respondents reported that the long term effects of relinquishment included their views about themselves, of other people, the role of father to the relinquished child, as well as their subsequent roles as husband or partner and as the father of other or later children. More than three-quarters (77%) of the birth fathers endorsed the statement: "There is part of me missing" (1993, p12) and acknowledged feelings of guilt, regret, sorrow and a frustration that the past mistake could not be undone. They also referred frequently to giving up responsibility ("and that was wrong"), of regretting letting down the mother and the child (*ibid*).

The men in Clapton's study, in response to the question: "What do you feel when you think of your child?", highlighted curiosity ("I'd just like to know what had happened to him, where he'd been, what he'd done"), concern or worry ("I worry about how abandoned she feels. Is she alive even?") and responsibility ("... there is also a certain sense of duty ... I very much want to be available for her" and "I still have all the parental feelings. They won't go away. It's a burden you can never put down") (2003, pp130–133). A feelings-based perspective of fatherhood emerges from this study:

> "Despite these men having had no experience of day-to-day care and having never seen the child since its birth some 30 years previously (and in some cases not even this visual

contact had taken place), the child remained in their minds. A bond with their adopted child seemed to run through these birth fathers' lives ... – out of sight has not meant out of mind. This study has shown that a man's feelings may not necessarily be engendered by social care and activity alone ... many of the men in this study felt an affectional bond, which some described as a parental feeling, with the child" (Clapton, 2003, pp186–187).

In the study conducted by Passmore and Coles, the participating birth fathers were asked to indicate the feelings that they had experienced about the adoption of their child since it took place. The findings are similar to those reported above by Clapton (2003). To quote Passmore and Coles, "The most common feeling was a sense of curiosity about their child ($n = 12$). For example, participants said they often thought about their child and wondered how he/she had fared in life, who he/she resembled, and whether the adoptive parents had treated their child well. One birth father also wondered if his child thought about the birth parents. Some birth fathers ($n = 3$) were also concerned about the welfare of the birth mother and wondered how she had fared" (2008, p7). As with previous studies, *eg* Schaefer (1991), Tugendhat (1992) and Cicchini (1993), guilt features prominently in the responses collected by Passmore and Coles: "After curiosity, guilt was the next most common feeling ($n = 10$), ranging from one birth father who said he had experienced "profound guilt" to another who indicated that he probably had not felt guilty enough. Abandonment of mother and child and failure to provide or take responsibility were the main reasons birth fathers gave for their feelings of guilt" (2008, p7).

Further undermining the popular image of the birth father as the swaggering sower of wild oats, is the documentation that records the permanent effect of adoption on their lives. As stated by Hart (2000), "Two myths were very alive in the world where he was living. One, that relinquishment was to be a buried secret. Two, that the adoption was a one-time event" (p14). Birth fathers

The Invisible Men of Adoption

speak eloquently of the lasting impact the loss of a child has had upon them. To quote Clapton (2001): "... experiences during the birth and adoption events constituted a milestone that had cast a long shadow and influence in the men's relationship with others, including subsequent partners and children, career choices and their opinion of themselves" (p5). Witney, in her study of sixty men who lost their infant children through adoption, reaches a similar conclusion. She reports that "The loss of power caused by their exclusion from the adoption process and by the inability to parent their children had unhappy ramifications throughout their lives, affecting fatherhood, marriage and self-esteem (2003, p12). Birth father Kevin (PARC, 1998) feels unable to forgive himself because he abandoned his infant child, therefore removing his daughter's "basic human right to know and be raised by her parents" (p21). In Cicchini (1993), one birth father, noting the effect relinquishment of his child has had on subsequent relationships, states: "I just can't start a good relationship with a woman. As soon as they get too close I walk away" (p12). Birth father Adam, whose correspondence with the daughter he was separated from by adoption is recorded in Saffian (1998), characterises his post-adoption period as "years of suppressed grief", marked by "somewhat self-destructive behavior" (p154). Mason (1995) comments that the loss of the child profoundly affects birth fathers in such areas as intimacy, trust and the realisation of goals and dreams (p22). "Losing a child is a life-altering, chronic grief situation" for birth fathers, she concludes (Mason, 1997, p17).

Fessler reported that lives of the "boyfriends" of several of the birth mothers she interviewed "had been adversely affected by the pregnancy and the breakup." In a specific example, Connie III cited the birth father's response to the intervention of parents, who forbad the intended marriage, "He went through a period of extreme rage ... at that time I was his whole life and that had been taken from him" (2006, p75).

In the poignant story of her birth father, Jane Hart (2000) observed that: "My birth father now sees that he became more aloof to attaching, became more busy, and used a wall of anger to hide the vulnerable pain, loss and guilt he felt" (p13).

What is not a surprise is that the feelings reported by birth fathers mirror those expressed by birth mothers, albeit, for birth fathers, in terms of airing in public, with a lag of at least two decades.

For birth mothers, their emotional reaction to loss has been well documented, both anecdotally and in professional analyses. Robinson (2003), in summarising these findings in her book *Adoption and Loss: The Hidden Grief*, concludes that women who had relinquished a child experience disenfranchised grief, previously described by Doka (1989) as the grief connected with a loss, which cannot be openly acknowledged, publicly mourned or socially supported. Robinson (1997) states, that for birth mothers: "They have no rituals to assist the grief process. They are unable to achieve resolution because of the absence of finality involved in their loss. They are denied social supports. They have no opportunities to express their grief. Their grief is seriously affected by their feelings of guilt and shame" (p286). Protocol demands that their grief remain hidden. This is a grief resulting from a loss, which confusingly for the birth mother, may seem to be reversible, because of the possibility of reunion with the lost child.

Robinson (2003) notes: "The grief of the woman who has lost a child through adoption is a unique experience and differs in fundamental ways from other grief experiences. Although the fathers of children lost through adoption often grieve also ... their grief has its own qualities and is not the same as that of the woman who has physically carried her child, given birth and signed the adoption consent form" (p101). Despite this lack of a biological bond, highlighted also by Stiffler (1992), the anecdotal evidence collected by Cicchini (1993), Mason (1995), Clapton (2003) and Passmore and Coles (2008) suggests that birth fathers also suffer from a form of disenfranchised grief.

For example, it is rare for a birth father's impending fatherhood to be acknowledged. (After all, men do not carry

The Invisible Men of Adoption

physically the visible results of conception.) Nor is there social recognition that they have, in fact, suffered a loss of their own through adoption. As Wells (1994) puts it, "birth fathers experienced a double denial: emotional and cultural. Permission to grieve was even less likely to be accorded to the birth father, since he may well have been the focus of blame by both sets of parents" (p67). In common with birth mothers, birth fathers have spent many years hiding the fact that they fathered a child relinquished to adoption, fearing their family and friends may shun them if their secret was revealed. Also, shame and guilt may have prevented them from seeking community support. The wound remains open, the grief resolution in limbo, because the living child may still return.

For birth fathers, there is an additional burden. Whereas birth mothers felt a responsibility for their babies and an imperative to bow to the wishes of their parents, for some birth fathers, *eg* Steve (quoted above, in Woolmington, 1992) there is also the expected role of the wise male protector to fulfil. Where this has not been possible, birth fathers have felt disempowered, denied an essence of their maleness.

It is obvious that birth fathers suffered similar pressures as did birth mothers, because, after all, both inhabited the same social milieu. Birth fathers, in common with birth mothers, were immature and confused and dependent on parental approval. Just as women were stereotyped as being promiscuous for getting pregnant and then callous for giving their babies away, so too fathers have been stigmatised for being selfish and uncaring.

CHAPTER 3

And father makes three

"It is our responsibilities, not ourselves, that we should take seriously." –
Peter Ustinov

The disempowered birth father

We men attending the birth fathers' workshop at the adoption conference held near Christchurch, New Zealand in February 1998, concluded that our lack of influence over decisions affecting the adoption of our children had had a permanent influence on our lives. This loss of control we identified as disempowerment (Coles, 1998, p120).

Bob told us of his love for Mary, which resulted in the conception of a daughter out of wedlock. Bob was committed to standing by Mary, but all attempts to contact her directly and by telephone and letters were intercepted by one or other of the sets of parents, especially Mary's. He was made to feel that he was totally to blame for the situation and told unequivocally that he was not fit to marry Mary. Unable to break through this barrier of opprobrium and resentful of the parental interference, Bob left New Zealand and tried to start over again in Australia. He married and divorced another woman within eighteen months and led an itinerant, unsettled lifestyle, until ... after 23 years, he returned to New Zealand and happened to meet an about-to-be divorced Mary in the street. Bob and Mary's story does have a 'happy ending' of sorts, for they did marry and have achieved reunion with their daughter. However, the issues surrounding the parents

The Invisible Men of Adoption

taking over their lives and usurping the decision-making role when Mary was pregnant with their child, remain unresolved.

In their studies of the influence of adoption on birth fathers, Cicchini (1993) and Clapton (2000, 2001, 2003) highlight the number of fathers who were deliberately excluded from the decision to adopt their child. Clapton (2001) has this to say in summary: "The adoption experience was often regarded as a significant disempowering event in that some men spoke about having been excluded from the decision-making process, and, in certain cases, having been either banned from seeing the birth mother and child or ejected from hospital. This experience of disenfranchisement – undergone by men who, in most cases, were in their late teens – was felt to have had a negative influence on their subsequent lives" (p4). As one of the men, who was not consulted about the decision to adopt his child, put it, "I felt that we, I, had no choice. No option. I felt guilty. The impression was that this was nothing to do with me. I felt isolated" (Clapton, 2003, p94). In his study Clapton reports that nine of the thirty birth fathers were so disillusioned by their adoption experience that they made a conscious decision not to have any further children (although two did become step parents).

The impact of disempowerment on Bob and other birth fathers who have had personal decision-making usurped by others, is pervasive. Their self-worth has been undermined, as expressed by this birth father: "There was really a loss of self-esteem and I felt bad. I felt I had brought on this shame" (Blau, 1993, p124). Birth fathers feel guilty and fear the risk of exposure, of being perceived as being unmanly for eschewing responsibility. They have been found wanting when faced with a crisis. Attempts to explain the situation which resulted in them not standing by the mother of their child are often treated by a prejudicial community as pathetic excuses. For the men, it is safer to shut down, to keep the pain internalised, not to inflict their shameful secret upon others. This bottling up is augmented by the common male unwillingness to express emotions (beyond anger), which mirrors society's expectation that birth fathers do not deserve to have feelings about the loss of a child for whom they bear the burden of a shirked responsibility.

The expectation that birth fathers remain invisible has been reinforced historically by fathers not being required to add their consent for adoption to that provided by the mother, as well as their non-appearance on the original birth certificate (except in a minority of cases – for example, only 2% of original birth certificates issued in New South Wales, Australia, prior to the 1980s include the birth father's name). These actions reinforce the commonly held beliefs that, not only does the father not contribute to the heritage of his child, but also that he is not relevant to decisions made about the child's future. Birth fathers, through the implementation of disenfranchising adoption laws, are absent in the records and, as a result, are seen as uncaring. Change is occurring, however, an example being New South Wales, where the *Adoption Act 2000* requires that the consent to adopt be provided by both birth parents, irrespective of their marital status. The *Adoption Act Queensland (2009)* has provision, in the event that the birth father is not named, for 'reasonable steps' to be taken to establish his identity, so that the father becomes an active participant in the consent process.

In some jurisdictions, the appearance of the birth father's name on the original birth certificate has depended upon a decision made by the birth mother whether or not to name him. Placing this decision in the hands of the birth mother reinforces the notion that the birth father has devolved responsibility. Not only does this procedure dishonour the role birth fathers played in conceiving their child, but it also leaves the lingering impression that the father did not care enough about his child to insist that his name be recorded on the original birth certificate. This perception may be picked up later by the searching adopted person, when they discover a birth certificate with but one birth parent name, that of the mother. It is no wonder then that so many adopted persons are apprehensive about finding their birth father. He is unknown, in all senses. In many circumstances, where the birth father's name is not recorded on the original birth certificate, it is the birth mother who controls both the revelation of his identity and the possibility of a reunion between father and child. Again, the birth father is disempowered.

There are anecdotal data from New Zealand, which suggest that social workers and lawyers deliberately avoided involving the birth father, because by not including his consent, the adoption was simplified. As a consequence of this practice, only the birth mother is recorded on the birth certificate, which implies, through a 'not recorded' for the birth father, that she chose not to give his name. There are instances of 'not known' being entered, as a convenience not a fact. Seen from the perspective of the searching adult adopted person, not only was the birth father too uncaring to register his name, but also, by extension, he does not want to meet and to know his son or daughter.

Harkness (1991) raises the possibility of a snowball effect occurring. She writes: "While a birth mother may have censored information about herself or about the baby's father (usually out of fear that her baby might not be acceptable), the social worker in turn chose to record only the information that he or she felt was important and this is what would be passed on to the adoptive parents. Adoptive parents then chose what information to pass on to the adopted child and so the censoring process continued" (p12). It is unlikely that the reputation of the birth father was enhanced by this orchestrated suppression. In some cases he is likely to have disappeared from the narrative altogether.

Often, the absence of the birth father from the birth record represents his exclusion by others from the adoption process, rather than how he felt at the time about the mother and their child.

The report by the New South Wales Legislative Council, released in 2000 and entitled *Releasing the Past: Adoption Practices 1950–1998: Final Report*, contains ample anecdotal evidence of the disempowerment of birth fathers. About the recording of the father's name on the birth certificate and other records, the report notes: "The treatment of those fathers who

The Invisible Men of Adoption

took an interest was often poor and as most practitioners have acknowledged, very little consideration was given to their needs. Very little was done for fathers and they were rarely consulted" (p114). Birth fathers and birth mothers told the committee preparing the report that their wishes to have the name of the father recorded on the original birth certificate had been ignored. In some cases, birth mothers had not been informed of the requirement that the father's name be recorded. This caused distress, when discovered many years later, for both of the birth parents and the searching adopted person.

One birth father speaks of the attempts he made to gain access to his newborn child and the mother at the hospital: "My recollection of events at this time and the feelings this evoked in me were confusion, powerlessness, complete denial of my rights and lack of any information" (New South Wales Legislative Council, 2000, p112).

During pregnancy, some social workers argued "that young women needed to be protected from 'these men' " (New South Wales Legislative Council, 2000, p80), a sweeping prejudicial view that utterly denies the rights of the birth father. As noted by the committee: "Despite the good intentions of these young men, family members and professionals often treated them with disdain. Angry and resistant parents often prevented them from seeing their pregnant girlfriend" (p71). Other men, granted a concession of sorts, speak of being permitted to visit their pregnant girlfriend in maternity homes, but then of being discouraged by social workers and/or the girl's family from participating in decisions about the future of the baby.

The committee concludes that "while the reaction of some men to the pregnancy was to deny responsibility, other men attempted to provide support and comfort but were thwarted by the attitudes and actions of family members, doctors, social workers, nuns and other professionals" (New South Wales Legislative Council, 2000, p72). Further, the committee states: "The fathers were disregarded and very little was done to consult or involve them during the birth and the postnatal period ... this

The Invisible Men of Adoption

failure to acknowledge fathers was wrong and caused long-term harm to those involved. The failure to record the birth father's name ... has also caused pain and suffering to them and to other people, including adoptees" (p119).

Even when the father makes the effort to correct the birth record by having his name added retrospectively, some legislation, for example that of New Zealand, still does not allow him automatic access to the proof of his paternity, leaving him with no recourse but to argue that he is deserving of special consideration. This is a perpetuation of the undermining of a birth father's moral right, an erosive process, which for many, began soon after the conception of their child.

Double jeopardy

For birth fathers, the disempowerment and the pain are intensified by a social expectation that men demonstrate responsibility at all times. A man who does not exhibit this 'desirable' male quality may be deemed by society to have failed. Men are aware of this disapproval, which they often internalise as shame. For a birth father, his negligence is felt all the more keenly, for he has let down not one, but two persons. The birth father has withdrawn his support for the birth mother, whether it be his decision or one made for him. By association, he has also relinquished his child. He has left both of them susceptible to the legacies of the wounds resulting from the separation of mother and child at birth. The birth father has failed the responsibility test, not once, but twice – the repercussions of a single decision. As a consequence, the father too bears a wound, for double abandonment is the core of "the unspoken burden that birth fathers carry" (Coles, 2004, Frontispiece).

Birth fathers may suffer intensified feelings of remorse, for not only forsaking two people and causing collateral damage, but also for failing to fulfil the male stereotype, of undermining manhood. These emotions are often suppressed, because they are too difficult to address. I believe, because the loss involves not one, but two people, many birth fathers experience magnified shame and guilt, which they bury very deeply in their psyche, for perhaps decades, until they reach a time in their lives where maturity is accompanied by a capacity to accept responsibility for past actions and the impact of those actions on others. To quote one of the birth fathers in Cicchini's 1993 study, who was middle aged when he made the comment – "I feel guilty about abandoning her and the child" (p12). According to Cicchini (1993), who drew on the conclusions of studies undertaken by several psychologists, "the behavioural expression of responsibility should be found in that period of life associated with greater maturity – adulthood, and more specifically, the mid-life years" (p5). All but two of the thirty birth fathers who volunteered to share their experiences with Cicchini were aged 35 and over. They had reached the stage in their lives where they felt comfortable about acting responsibly. The same background studies referred to by Cicchini note that adolescent males and young men in their twenties are intent on finding and reinforcing their identity through occupational and social achievement. The subsequent orientation toward duty accompanies maturity. Clearly, on the subject of responsibility, the expectations of society about when a man should be responsible (always) and when a man feels comfortable about accepting responsibility for his actions, are misaligned.

    I contend that just as the shame of not displaying responsibility in late adolescence may produce profound denial, so the acquisition of responsibility in the middle-age years can result in a painful release of a birth father's suppressed feelings. The guilt of a double abandonment becomes concern for the well-being of not one but two persons. Two people were neglected then, two people have re-entered his thoughts. Birth fathers have the mother of their child, as well as the child, on their conscience. A birth father may relate to the term 'double jeopardy', in the sense that he has charged himself twice for the one act. This responsibility for altering the lives of two other persons is unique

The Invisible Men of Adoption

to birth fathers, as is their experience of a dual loss. This is reflected in Clapton's study: "... loss for some men included the possibility of a family life that would have included the birth mother and child" (2001, p5) and reinforced by Witney: "Most men lost not only their child but also their lover" (2003, p12). Michael, in Taylor (1995) is a birth father who grieves for the mother and their child. The birth mother reports: "While he suffered enormously due to the loss of his daughter to adoption, he also suffered more consciously than I regarding the loss of our relationship with each other" (p135) and later: "It became even more clear to me that Michael had suffered as much as I had over the course of the nineteen years our child was lost to us" (p287). Not only does the birth father lament the loss of his child, but his disenfranchised grief may embrace the birth mother as well. Socially, this complicates matters, because few in the community are likely to tolerate a birth father speaking of his residual feelings for the birth mother. The birth father who tells his story in an Australian collection of personal narratives reveals a matter that he admits he cannot share with his wife: "The thing that has been really hard is ... the loss of my ex-girlfriend [the birth mother of his daughter] out of my life " (NSW Committee on Adoption and Permanent Care, Inc, 2001, p43).

A birth mother may rue the departure of the birth father and at the very least be disappointed that he has not stood by her, but the bonding achieved through pregnancy and birth ensures that a birth mother's loss typically focuses on the child. [Note, my comments here relate only to the scope of the loss, not to the intensity of the resultant grief. My intention is to draw attention to the breadth of the adoption loss and grief experienced by birth fathers.]

Two in mind

Birth fathers experience a further complicating factor. Many never saw the child they forsook. For these men, their primary relationship was with the birth mother. If his feelings for her were strong, he may believe she is the primary victim of his lack of responsibility. Witness this birth father from Cicchini's 1993 study: "Because of my abandonment of the mother I felt and still feel guilty" (p13). These are the words of a man who has 'unfinished business', as depicted in the Adoption Sandwich. As a result of this prioritisation, a birth father's shame and guilt may centre initially on the birth mother and then subsequently on their child. The child may not be the focal point of his neglect. This hierarchy may affect the sequence in which he deals with his pain. Making peace with the birth mother may be his priority. An outcome of this prioritisation is that the birth father may feel doubly guilty about placing his child second.

Just as the quality of the relationship between the two birth parents during the conception, birth and adoption of their child may influence a birth mother's response to the child's (as an adult) request for information about the father, so in a similar manner may the primary focus of a birth father's search be affected. If, prior to the adoption, the birth mother and birth father were close and he is remorseful about the circumstances of their parting, then possibly she will be uppermost in his thoughts as he contemplates reconciliation. Whether or not he saw his child after the birth may also guide his reactions. A father who held his child is perhaps more likely to put son or daughter first. However, for some birth fathers, where they had forged a strong attachment with both mother and child, or neither of them, the decision to search may create confusion. Concurrent searches consume much effort and emotional energy and create their own ambivalence, so sequential searches are more manageable. But who to place first – the birth mother or their child? This is a dilemma for some birth fathers. For other birth fathers, the decision is made for them. To get information about their child, they may seek the assistance of the birth mother. In other circumstances, the adult child may find the father, as either the first birth parent approached, or more typically, after the birth mother. Research has shown that most birth fathers welcome the inclusion of their child in their lives, even if some men take a little time to become used to the change. In this circumstance, where the birth father has been contacted, then his relationship building is naturally focused on his child. During the course of getting to know his son or daughter, the subject of the birth mother will certainly arise. For the birth father, again depending on the quality of his initial relationship with the birth mother and the status of his present feelings about her, this may cause him angst as he recalls the past and he allows buried emotions to emerge. If he acknowledges his guilt at forsaking the birth mother, he is likely to want to seek conciliation with her.

Clapton (2003) concludes that, based on his study, the birth father continues to think about and have feelings for the birth mother. "Of the 21 men who parted with the birth mother, 16 had contact with her after the adoption" (p142). Significantly, a third of this group, *ie* seven, reported "strong positive feelings for the birth mother" 25 to 30 years after the adoption took place (p143). These are men who feel they have 'unfinished business'. Clapton does not comment on the timing or the duration of the contacts, nor does he investigate the basis for these lasting and influential feelings – whether, for example they correspond with the quality of the relationship between the birth parents at the time of the birth and the adoption, or are connected perhaps to the birth father wanting to apologise to the birth mother for having wronged her. Given that Clapton and other researchers have commented on how common it is for the birth parents to have been 'going steady' prior to the pregnancy, birth and adoption, it may be anticipated that lingering feelings exist. Whilst both parents may have residual affectional feelings for the other, a birth father's may be complicated by guilt. If the birth father has acknowledged the consequences of feeling he is a double abandoner, the presence of the birth mother in his thoughts is to be expected. This would reinforce the observation that a birth father may be concerned about the well-being of the mother <u>and</u> the child, years, even decades after the adoption. According to Clapton (2003), later-life contact has not been reported in studies of birth mothers' post-adoption experiences. This could be because, perhaps, few birth mothers have initiated resumed contact with the birth father. It is unlikely that an 'abandoned' woman will have the same imperative to seek reconciliation as the man who feels guilty about abandoning her.

Whilst the birth mother's responses to 'unfinished business' may range from anger to a pining for what might have been, her reaction is unlikely to include guilt over the loss of the birth father, except when she feels that she did not defend him and their relationship against his banishment by her parents. It is difficult to envisage the birth mother being labelled a double abandoner (unless she has lost more than one child through adoption). It is the birth father, alone, who bears the guilt of abandoning an adult and a child. An errant arrow launched by the father has hit and wounded the other members of his 'birth family'. It is birth fathers who experience difficulties living up to Kahlil Gibran's metaphor of the parent as the stable bow, just as birth mothers bear the guilt of not living up to society's expectations that they fulfil the role of the primary, dedicated, nurturing parent.

The Triple Bond

Birth fathers who have spoken out have exhibited a willingness to own up to the damage caused to themselves, the child they lost through adoption and the mother of the child. Birth fathers' reactions to loss, as it applies to the child have been documented in the studies undertaken by Cicchini (1993), Clapton (2003) and Passmore and Coles (2008). That fathers have feelings about the birth mother has been touched upon, but hitherto, not explored in depth.

I contend that for the birth father who, in particular, was excluded from supporting the birth mother prior to the adoption, his natural response is a deep regret for having let her down. He may not have articulated this at the time (if indeed the opportunity arose), but it is unlikely that his concerns will have evaporated. Indeed, it is plausible that, with maturity and an allied willingness to deal with the past, his admission of personal pain and the impact of his neglect may occur many years after the event that caused the wounds. It is no surprise then that the birth mother can remain in the mind of the birth father. Such an outcome may be anticipated, particularly if the adoption severed a significant relationship between the birth parents.

The Adoption Sandwich depicts the bonds that exist between the birth mother and her child. It also displays, based on Stiffler (1992), the lesser bonds between the birth father and the same child. Seen from the perspective of the birth father, there is also a third bond that may be present – the affectional bond between the birth father and the birth mother, beyond conception. It is this bond, tinged with guilt, which is the foundation of any 'unfinished business' that a birth father may have.

This overall network, which I term the Triple Bond, has broader ramifications. Not only are birth mother, child and birth father linked by fundamental relationship factors, but also by the wounds created by the adoption. The benefits of working collaboratively to heal these wounds are discussed in later chapters.

CHAPTER 4

Finding the father within

"The real voyage of discovery consists not in seeking new landscapes but in having new eyes." – Marcel Proust

Kaplan and Silverstein (1991) write of the seven core issues in adoption, as they apply to adopted persons, birth parents (in their case, the mother) and adoptive parents. Taking into account personal knowledge and the reactions recorded in, for example, Cicchini (1993), Mason (1995) Clapton (2003) and Passmore and Coles (2008), I have used this framework to record the experiences of birth fathers. The setting is closed adoptions that took place in the post World War II period:

- ***Loss***: Ruminate about the lost child – feel something is missing from our lives. May rue broken relationship with birth mother. Feel unable to articulate our loss(es); if do so, may be consigned to social isolation.
- ***Rejection***: Reprimand selves as being irresponsible and unworthy, because have permitted adoption. As a result, keep illegitimacy and adoption a secret, because fear community's negative reaction. Should we seek reunion, fear reprobation by the child we feel we abandoned (this is our greatest fear).
- ***Guilt/Shame***: Party to a guilty secret. Feel shame and guilt for negligent actions, which resulted in the child being placed for adoption and caused damage to a mother's life.
- ***Grief***: No rituals for mourning; grief resolution is delayed and disenfranchised. The right of the birth father to grieve the loss

of his child (and perhaps the birth mother) may not be recognised by the community, because of a perception that he is selfish and uncaring.
- ***Identity***: Lose part of identity as the procreating father. Confusion about whether or not can call ourselves a parent, because we let a child go. Difficulty in responding truthfully when asked how many children we have. May feel invisible and undeserving of recognition if unacknowledged on our child's original birth certificate.
- ***Intimacy***: Wary of intimacy, because it may lead to another loss. Unresolved issues with the birth mother may interfere with future relationships.
- ***Control***: Relinquishment of a child seen as having yielded control to internal fears and external influences. It is a disempowering, life-changing event. Outcome may be self-imposed control, as a strategy to deny effects of the separation caused by the adoption.

These reactions, with varying degrees of emphasis, apply to the three categories of birth father whom Lifton (1988, pp158–160) identifies as showing concern for the well-being of their child. The 'Missing Father' and the 'Ambivalent Father' may suffer from unresolved guilt and/or denial and the 'Father Who Cares' is the man who has had control wrested from him by persons exercising authority.

Every person adopted has a birth mother and a birth father. For every birth mother there is a birth father. Yet, by any reckoning, birth fathers' participation in the adoption experience is minimal. This statement holds true whether the criterion is being named on the birth certificate, participation in the process of consent to adopt, initiating reunion with the lost child, being the primary subject of a search, or attending adoption support group meetings and conferences (to present the birth father viewpoint and so become instruments of change). For too long the voice of the birth father has been passive. Under the banner of birth parents, we have allowed birth mothers to assume the role of representing our views. Accordingly, we are often referred to in passing, because there is a lack of hard data about us. Further, a tacit assumption is made that any feelings we may have, are but a diminished version of the well documented birth mother reactions to adoption and loss. Whilst birth fathers' feelings do to some extent mirror those expressed by birth mothers, the birth father view contains some unique qualities. I contend that these centre on recognising and processing the:

- historical social neglect of the birth father,
- compounded internal guilt caused by our abandonment of mother and child, of consigning two people to their fates, and
- delayed acceptance of responsibility for our actions, fuelled by a male reluctance to admit to and express feelings.

These factors often combine, so that the birth father may enter a period of numbness after the birth of his child. This may result from his deep shame, reinforced by the blame formerly thrust upon him by his and the birth mother's parents, and perhaps the birth mother, as well as the consequent difficulties he has with communicating his feelings to an unsympathetic community. Moving to more prosaic matters, such as focusing on a career, may seem a safe haven. It is through maturity that many men in the mid-span of their years embrace duty and begin looking inwards at what they think about themselves and their place in the world. It is then that they may acknowledge the impact their earlier actions potentially had on others and on themselves. It is the degree to which a birth father processes and communicates these insights that influences how he is perceived now by the birth mother, their adult child and by himself. There is evidence that even when men did not know that they had fathered a child, they react positively in middle age to being surprised by their adult adopted son or daughter. Whatever a birth father's belated accomplishments, undoubtedly there will be birth mothers and adopted persons who wish he had displayed responsibility when they needed him to, perhaps decades earlier.

The Invisible Men of Adoption

Whilst the empirical investigations made by Cicchini (1993) and Clapton (2001, 2003) have produced important findings, hitherto they have not been drawn together and given a broader perspective. Cicchini's conclusion that responsibility evolves with maturity is a critical contribution to the understanding of birth fathers' actions and reactions over time. Clapton's (2003, p142) observation that a significant proportion of birth fathers retain positive feelings for the birth mother is also important. When these salient points are combined, they reinforce the complexity and the uniqueness of the birth father experience. A birth father may rue the loss of a child, as well as a broken relationship with the birth mother, complicating his adoption experience. He may feel the impact of a dual loss as well as guilt associated with failing two persons to whom he is intimately connected – the mother and their child. Further, he may feel burdened by the realisation that he has not fulfilled the traditional role expected of him, that of the reliable protector/provider of a family. There is evidence, even in situations where a man is unaware he has fathered a child who was adopted, that being found by his adult son or daughter is accompanied by a delayed activation of guilt. The maturity factor may contribute to these feelings emerging or intensifying over time. Add in the ingredients of disempowerment and social stereotyping as further influences and the birth father begins to acquire substance and moreover, a presence as a discrete birth parent.

Informed by personal involvement and drawing upon the results of the studies, a broad picture of birth fathers evolves. This is summarised as 'The Birth Father Experience' (see Figure 2 below). This overview embraces the social setting, and within the three phases of a birth father's experiential continuum, summarises the key actions and reactions. The role of control is highlighted where its effects are palpable. Birth mothers may notice certain similarities to their own experiences, particularly others deciding 'what was best for their child' *ie* adoption, their personal reactions to the loss of a child and their feelings about the child, as well as the advantages of searching and the reunion.

Figure 2: The Birth Father Experience – An Overview

Male Traditional Role: Protector/Provider

Community Expectations: That men demonstrate responsibility at all times

1. Conception, Pregnancy, Birth and Adoption [months]

Internal = Self	External = Others
Avoidance – Denial of responsibility for paternity	Involvement blocked by birth parents' parents/birth mother/Social Workers ***(External locus of Control – Circle of Concern)***

2. Post-Adoption [years]

Emergent, maintained or intensified feelings about:

Self	Child	Birth mother
Self-esteem	Curiosity	'Unfinished business'
Disenfranchised grief	Concern for his/her well-being	Concern for her well-being
Shame – failing to fulfil expected role, thus forsaking mother and child	Guilt – letting child go, not fulfilling parental role	Guilt – not being there for her when she needed him
Personal identity	Connectedness	

3. Search and reunion (where initiated by the birth father) [years]

Reconciliation with:

Self	Adult child, birth mother
Triggered by an acceptance of responsibility for past actions, often a product of maturity – with positive consequences for the other members of the family of origin	Represents acknowledgment that adoption causes damage to the three members of a family of origin and that, with the willing participation of all, a measure of healing (= grief resolution) is possible for each person. For the birth father, seeking an accord with both birth mother and child may be very important; hence a triadic search and reunion, as a consequence of the Triple Bond

(Internal locus of Control – Circle of Influence)

The Invisible Men of Adoption

What this table does reinforce is what differentiates the birth father experience – the influence of responsibility on his actions, against the community's expectations of fatherhood, and his dual focus on mother and child.

For a man who experiences the burden of double abandonment, of feeling that he has let down two people, processing his feelings, searching and reunion is likely to be complex. The leading players in a birth mother's search and reunion are typically her child and herself. A birth father's search and reunion experience may involve, for him, a necessary reconciliation with both the birth mother and their adult child. In other words, for a birth father the search and reunion 'model' may be a triad, whereas for a birth mother it is more likely to be the dyad. Adopted persons' stories of search and reunion are more often aligned with the 'model' for birth mothers, in the sense that for adopted persons the birth mother is typically the primary (and sometimes the sole) objective of their search.

Overcoming the barriers (external)

The birth father view deserves to be heard and validated. But how can birth fathers project themselves? There are two perspectives, one external to the birth father, the other internal. It is true that today birth fathers can participate in the decision to give up a child to adoption, in situations where this is enshrined in the legislation. However, legislation in isolation cannot drive change, as evidenced by the experience in Victoria, where some mothers still refuse to name the father of their child, despite inclusion being the intent of the Act. Here the old attitude toward birth fathers has not been stamped out by the enactment of law.

Clearly, a fundamental change to the way birth fathers are viewed is required. Certainly birth fathers can assist their cause by becoming more vocal and expressing their views. However, birth fathers need to feel that their viewpoint will be respected before they feel comfortable about speaking out. What can be done to smooth the way? The key is eroding the disempowerment, which traditionally has been the lot of birth fathers.

In New Zealand, where my son was born, those birth fathers who played no role in the placement of their child are still prohibited from accessing their child's original birth certificate. Under current legislation in that country, only the adult adopted person may apply for their original birth certificate. Birth parents are excluded, unless they obtain a copy of the certificate from their child (in a situation where reunion has occurred), or, if, as in my case, they plead special consideration from the Family Court. This inequity denies birth parents the right to access proof of their parenthood. It perpetuates the myth that the birth father and the birth mother did not conceive and bring a child into the world. To all but the zealous bureaucratic protectors of these records, the birth parents do not exist. They are disenfranchised.

Giving the birth father unfettered access to the official recognition of his part in the conception of his child would be a step forward, for it allows him to validate himself and his role. Birth fathers can aid their own cause here. Even if they were not recorded on the birth certificate when their child was born, it is in their own interests to arrange to have their name added retrospectively. One of the men in Passmore and Coles' 2008 study stated his reason for taking the trouble, several years later, to insert his name: "I wanted my son to know the name of his birth father."

Belated admission of paternity may of necessity involve seeking the approval of the birth mother, thus creating an opportunity for a rapprochement. (Some jurisdictions, such as New Zealand and South Australia, allow the birth father to be registered as the male parent if he is noted in their records or he matches identifying descriptive data.) With the recording of the father on the birth certificate, the adopted person then officially has two birth parents. They now 'belong' in three families, those of their adoptive parents, their birth mother and their birth father. I welcome Robinson's acknowledgment of the importance of the birth father, recorded in the Introduction of the revised edition of

The Invisible Men of Adoption

her book *Adoption and Loss: The Hidden Grief* (2003). She writes: "Every baby born into the world becomes a member of two families; the family of the mother and the family of the father. If the child is subsequently adopted, then the adoptive family becomes that child's third family." Despite these relationship tangibles, she is concerned "that while many mothers now realise that they lost their children through adoption because they were misinformed, disempowered and afraid, some have not yet been able to acknowledge that the fathers of their children may have been similarly disadvantaged." Robinson (*ibid*) concludes: "I hope that ... more mothers will appreciate the role they can play in assisting and supporting their children to make contact with their fathers." I agree, wholeheartedly.

Through reunion, the father contributes a significant benefit to his child. He provides a conduit to identity settlement for his son or daughter. Another asset that a birth father brings to reunion is his availability to answer questions about the circumstances of his child's conception and relinquishment to adoption. This dialogue may contribute to the healing of three parties, the adopted person, the birth mother and the birth father himself.

Birth fathers need not maintain play a passive role, *ie* as the second parent, sometimes sought. There is abundant evidence that adopted persons welcome contact initiated by their birth fathers.

For a birth father who takes the initiative to locate his child, searching and ultimately, reunion, are two sequentially linked means by which he may seek to recover the personal control that perhaps was wrested from him at the time his child was adopted. The search becomes a quest for discovering both a part of his identity and the descendant he was separated from by adoption. Whilst that which was lost cannot be returned, each piece of information collected during the search phase assumes a gem-like quality, as it brings the adopted person closer. A picture of the person he has missed nurturing and watching grow up begins to emerge, like a butterfly from a chrysalis. His 'child' begins to assume an identity. The product of his genes has substance as a living person.

The Invisible Men of Adoption

Addressing personal adoption issues, whether from the perspective of a birth parent or an adopted person, is a commitment to a journey of discovery. Two quotes from Robinson illustrate this perfectly, *viz*, "... it's not forgetting your lost child that allows you to get on with your life, but remembering him" (2003, p48) and from her son, "Every adopted person should search for their natural parents ... how can you ever expect to truly know yourself if you never know your natural parents?" (2000a, p207). We, as persons whose lives have been affected by adoption, appreciate any assistance and a legislatively sanctioned veto that prevents access to information or prohibits contact represents an unwelcome and unnecessary barrier to the achievement of self-awareness. Whereas other adults in the community can make choices regarding their relationships, the veto denies birth parents and adopted persons the capacity to forge a relationship, a demeaning situation based solely on the circumstance of birth.

Overcoming the barriers (internal)

For birth fathers, internal matters can be more difficult to resolve. Often, men are uncomfortable with expressing their feelings. If any display of male emotion is anticipated, then it is of anger, which sometimes masks other suppressed feelings. Men are not encouraged to exhibit profound sadness, nor show fear or guilt.

The wisdom of men suppressing their feelings has been challenged in numerous recent publications. Steve Biddulph (1994) begins his book *Manhood* with these words: "Most men don't have a life. Instead, we have just learned to pretend. Much of what men do is an outer show, kept up for protection" (p1). He then draws the distinction between the genders: "Most women today are not like this. They act from inner feeling and spirit, and more and more they know *who they are* and *what they want*" (*ibid*). A little further on, Biddulph explores these differences in more detail:

The Invisible Men of Adoption

" Women had to overcome *oppression*, but men's difficulties are with *isolation*. The enemies, the prisons from which men must escape are:
– loneliness,
– compulsive competition, and
– lifelong emotional timidity.

Women's enemies are largely in the world around them. Men's enemies are often on the inside – in the walls we put up around our hearts. The inner changes will have to come first ... Coming out from behind these walls (slowly, carefully) will mean that men can change and grow – to our own benefit and to the great benefit of women and children" (p4).

On the final page of *Manhood*, Biddulph concludes: "The key is to *let your feelings out*" (p196) [emphases in the reference].

Psychologist Claude Riedel, writing in Mason (1995) suggests that birth fathers often keep their fatherhood a secret, because of shame. He goes on: "Not speaking about the experience shuts down the grief process in its early stages and negatively impacts (*sic*) the development of trust, identity, intimacy, sexuality and self-esteem ... To break out of this cycle, the birthfather must name, remember and redefine his experience" (pp264–265).

If birth fathers choose to remain silent, they face an additional risk; the community remains uninformed about what it means to be a birth father. In such circumstances, it is likely that the damaging stereotype of the birth father as the callous man who fled and is forever detached from the birth, the adoption and the well-being of his child will remain, unchallenged. When in 2003, the Adoption Research & Counselling Service in Western Australia tried to organise workshops to help others in the adoption community understand the experiences of birth fathers, they discovered that this traditional view prevailed. As reported by Jennifer Newbould: "The message we overwhelmingly had from adoptive parents and birthmothers was of the irrelevance of the birthfather – and a belief in the myth that these fathers don't care and that the adopted person is only interested in contact/information about their birthmother." She continues: "We have a long way to go to redress these false assumptions and the implications these stereotypes have for adopted children/adults" (Newbould, 2003, p2). However, concludes Newbould, men do care, but are wary about how they are perceived: "[Birthfathers] who contacted us about the workshop had not shared their story, had not forgotten their child, did feel grief about their loss, felt guilt, but despite all these feelings did not feel any entitlement to have their feelings considered" (*ibid*).

Birth mothers can vouch for the impact of stigmatisation. For decades, they laboured under the public's misconception that they had willingly given up their children to adoptive parents, put the event behind them and 'got on with the rest of their lives'. For birth mothers, it took a concerted campaign, characterised by emotional honesty, to destroy these myths and create an accurate picture of what it means to be a woman who lost a child through adoption. Just as birth mothers showed courage to reveal these truths, thus confronting how they were perceived by others (and the way they felt about themselves), so birth fathers must be prepared to be vulnerable and to mount their own offensive. Otherwise, the men who lost children through adoption will continue to be misrepresented.

For men, admission and integration seem to be more difficult than for women. In part at least, this may be because of conditioning. Many men and women believe that adult males are expected to be physically strong, emotionally contained, independent, cool in a crisis and a bulwark.

However, emotionally contained is not the same as emotionally repressed. Containment embodies control, whereas repression invokes a deliberate shutting down. Many men are more comfortable with the latter, because they believe that a display of anaesthetised inner strength is the appropriate counter to the threat of an unwelcome assault on their emotional shield. Some men use the secure haven of sport (as participants or spectators) as a diversion and the outlet for feelings such as loyalty, disappointment, exhilaration and anger. Ultimately, men's fear of expressing themselves emotionally may, for many, be related to a fundamental misgiving that by revealing their feelings, they risk losing the essence of their masculinity – the respected qualities of being rational, taciturn, disciplined and impregnable will be undermined.

Through socialisation, many men have been cut off from their feelings. Although, as a community, we have announced that we accept men who express emotions (excluding uncontrolled anger), for a myriad of men there are generations of stereotyping to overcome.

I know, from personal experience and witnessing other birth fathers in Australia, New Zealand and the United States that the internal male barrier related to the communication of feelings can be overcome, with positive results not only for the men who have made the effort, but also for those within their circles of influence. Making the change, radical for many men, certainly takes courage. Reaching in, ultimately to give, in the spirit of openness, has to be a heartfelt action, or else the exposure of emotions will wither, not blossom, and with it the capacity of men to know their whole selves

Out of the shadows

That birth fathers do have strong feelings about their adoption experiences is amply demonstrated by those men who have contributed to the studies conducted by Deykin *et al* (1988), Cicchini (1993), Clapton (2003) and Passmore and Coles (2008). However, these men are but a small sampling of those fathers who have lost children through adoption. What the published results have in common is that the birth fathers whose views were sought were visible – they have been or had indicated a wish to be in contact with their child and are willing to share their adoption and post-adoption experiences. In common with studies involving birth mothers, adopted persons and adoptive parents, the voice is that of the surveys' participants, not the grouping as a whole. Whilst it is encouraging that these men have come forward, the key is to entice more birth fathers to have their say. For this to occur, birth fathers need to feel comfortable that their concerns, when expressed, are acknowledged and validated by birth mothers, adopted persons, adoptive parents and social workers. Birth father Randy Wood is one who has spoken on this topic. He refers to "the men of character we need to become for our children and our children's birthmothers", facilitated by a requirement that "others reach out to birthfathers and help them find a path out of the shadows so they can mend" (Wood, 2002, p8).

Many birth fathers remain reticent about revealing their past and exposing deep-seated emotions. These are men who need to make a special personal effort and require also the forgiveness of a community that once shunned them. Thankfully, there are some birth fathers who have felt moved to overcome the original stigma, which was attached to them by a society that disapproved of both their actions and inaction. These men have set a fine example.

CHAPTER 5

The fortunate minority

"A man cannot be comfortable without his own approval." — Mark Twain

Preamble

In her thesis, Stromberg writes: "The shift [over the past twenty years] from closed to open adoptions has had a significant impact on the role of birth fathers in adoption. Open adoption has allowed birth fathers more of an opportunity to not only participate in the adoption plan for their child, but to sustain a relationship with their child over the years that follow" (2002, p77). Whilst I welcome this increased involvement of birth fathers in recent times, my focus is upon the majority of birth fathers who are the product of that earlier era, when freedom of interpersonal contact was denied in the aftermath of an adoption.

The absent men

At the 7th, 8th and 9th Australian Adoption Conferences, I was the only birth father among a combined total of more than 600 attendees. I did not feel out of place or unwelcome. Rather, my involvement was commented upon favourably by the overwhelmingly female gatherings. However, the question I find myself asking is, "Where are all the birth fathers?"

The invisibility of birth fathers has been confirmed for me elsewhere. Articles written by journalists about my experience

The Invisible Men of Adoption

have appeared in the press. I have told my story and shared my findings about the impact of adoption on birth fathers over the radio, yet in almost every case, it is others with adoption experiences, not birth fathers, who have corresponded with me. The response to a summary of my adoption story, which appeared in *The Age* on Father's Day in 2002, is illuminating. Of the four men who asked me to contact them, one was an old school friend. When I followed up with the other three men, all, I discovered, were birth fathers. Their responses were fascinating and perhaps representative. One welcomed contact and we met subsequently. A second birth father arranged to meet me, but did not keep the appointment. When I called him later, he admitted that he had defaulted, because he had realised he was not yet ready to share his adoption experience. The third birth father said he was 'still thinking about it' and would call me when he was ready. I have not heard from him since.

When I toured New Zealand in late 2004, only two birth fathers attended the five seminars Evelyn Robinson and I presented jointly in four cities. They were among the approximately 10 per cent of men, overall, who attended the gatherings. One of the birth fathers observed that he had found that once he began sharing his adoption experience with others, his circle of friends changed. He now spent less time with men, but had broadened his range of female acquaintances. He told me that other men had questioned the wisdom of his acknowledgment of the past. Under an open adoption arrangement, the other (younger) birth father maintained regular contact with his child and the adoptive parents. He found it somewhat difficult to relate to the experiences of birth fathers who have been separated from their children for decades, but he acknowledged at the end of my presentation that his eyes had been opened.

In Australia, since the mid-1960s there have been approximately 70,000 local placements to adoptive parents who are strangers to the child. This means there are, give or take a few, for multiple paternity and death, as a minimum, an equivalent number of birth fathers alive today in Australia. Men who

The Invisible Men of Adoption

conceived a child forty years ago, would, now, in general, be in their early sixties. There are likely to be, given the number of adoptions that occurred in the twenty years immediately following World War II (before the peak years of the late sixties and early seventies), additional birth fathers living from this earlier period, supplementing the 70,000 referred to above. In the United States, the 2000 census recorded over seven million adopted persons (Griffith, personal communication, 2005). These are the children of an equivalent number of birth fathers. How is it then that birth fathers are nigh but invisible to the public?

That birth fathers were historically not required to be recorded on the original birth certificate provides a partial answer. We know that some of these fathers were not informed by the birth mother of their paternity, either to protect the man (for example, he may already have been married) or because he may have been a person she did not wish to have identified as her child's progenitor.

These arguments may work for ephemeral relationships between the birth mother and the birth father, but another response is required for the frequent long term relationships that an adoption interrupted (reported separately by Harkness (1991), Nicholls and Levy (1992), Carlini (1993), Clapton (2003), Witney (2003) and Passmore and Coles (2008)). Birth fathers who have maintained strong feelings for the birth mother are unlikely to have forgotten the events surrounding the adoption and the consequences for the child and both birth parents. One might expect these to be the fathers who, even if they did not see their child, would later try to locate the birth mother, to determine her welfare. Yet these men have not, with infrequent exceptions, been forthcoming. Why?

Perhaps there are clues from studies that have focussed not on birth fathers, but other participants, when addressing post-adoption issues. According to Jones, for birth mothers, "Having evaluated the available resources, most concluded that *only* other birthmothers could understand their feelings or problems; many were unable to trust or confide in anyone else" (1993, p140). The implication here is that birth mothers' healing is aided by the empathy of other birth mothers. This need for validation, applied to birth fathers, is reinforced by Gediman and Brown: "In circles where birthfathers feel more or less comfortable, one can hear men admit to feeling 'guilty as hell' that they didn't come through for their [children] or [the birth mothers]" (1991, p183). This last comment is helpful. Whilst birth fathers may feel guilty about not being there for the birth mother and their child, they may be unwilling to share their feelings amongst other birth mothers and adopted persons, people whom they believe could judge them harshly. Further, because men often internalise their feelings, a birth father may not be aware that there are other birth fathers who share his responses to loss. He may believe he is an island in a sea of male peer indifference.

Birth fathers are under-represented in studies about the impact of adoption on the members of the family of origin. This is in part a reflection of the general unwillingness of birth fathers to come forward. I suspect that, for several reasons, the majority of birth fathers do not make themselves available in the aftermath of an adoption. Some are unaware of their status. Others prefer to continue to deny that they fathered a child who was adopted. Many feel that they are not ready to explore and share their adoption issues. I believe that these factors conspire to keep a comprehensive birth father view suppressed. Those birth fathers who are represented in published studies typically have addressed, at least to some degree, how they feel about their adoption experiences. I maintain that these men are the fortunate minority.

The traditional societal view of the birth father is that he is the feckless lothario. Other persons with adoption experiences are also members of the community. They may both reflect and contribute to the stereotype that surrounds the birth father. Adopted persons, in particular, looking for any image of the birth father, may internalise the general view and this can have a negative effect on how they view the man they have never met

The Invisible Men of Adoption

– they may assume that he fits the popular perception and consider that he is not worth knowing.

In the study by Howarth, which records the stories of adopted persons, there is a high proportion of searchers who included the birth father in their quest. Howarth relates this to the "many adoptees who believe they have a right to knowledge of their origins, both through contact with their birth mother *and* father, regardless of the circumstances surrounding their conception and birth" (1988, p183) [emphasis in the original]. From an earlier source, written from the perspective of an adopted person who found her birth father after more than forty years of effort, Florence Fisher says, "This was my natural father, and finding him more than justified the unspeakable search that had occupied almost my whole life" (1973, p20).

Regrettably, this consideration of the birth father is not repeated in publications that post-date Howarth. Perhaps the view of one of the adopted persons in her book is still a factor that discourages some adopted persons. David says he has no desire for contact with his birth father and defends his personal position with: "Why should I? ... fifteen minutes versus nine months" (1988, p93). David's view is unhelpful. Not only does he assume that his birth father fits the mould of the man who has his sport and moves on, but he also implies another element of the stereotype – the man is the villain and the birth mother is the victim.

Zara Phillips (2004) presents a contrary viewpoint. She battles her (birth) mother's lack of understanding of her, Zara's, need to know her birth father. Phillips asserts that establishing the father–daughter connection is as important to her as knowing Pat, the mother. "I miss not knowing what he looks like, who he is, what kind of man he is ..." (p126) and "I am sometimes jealous of others who have spent time with their [birth] fathers" (p147).

The Invisible Men of Adoption

Overcoming the hurdles

The common male reluctance to share feelings and to admit to shortcomings, coupled with guilt, compounded because he has affected the lives of the mother and the child, is a barrier that some birth fathers feel they are unable to surmount. This shield can prevent progress, because it affects not only how these birth fathers feel about themselves, but also their capacity to convey their concerns to others. Often, a birth father's defence may be to deny all feelings about the adoption and its consequences, simply because this strategy seems more manageable and less risky. This reaction is less common amongst birth mothers, who seem to realise that progress is not possible without opening up emotionally, to themselves and to the community. If few men are willing to be transparent about their adoption experiences, then, for example, it is not surprising that birth fathers find it difficult to start, let alone maintain support groups. This however, does not imply that birth fathers are condemned to isolation and denial. It does mean that men may have to dedicate time and effort to overcoming the inhibitors that lie largely within themselves.

That men often do not express their feelings is echoed by a newspaper article about men's experiences of in-vitro fertilisation treatment (*The Age,* 3 October 2004). One father involved in the programme comments that "in more than five years' involvement with IVF, he had never heard another man even raise the subject of male infertility, let alone men's feelings." In an echo of the often-heard comment about adoption, IVF is considered to be 'women's business'.

Robinson points out that parents may feel differently about the child they lost to adoption, depending on whether the adopted person is still a minor or has become an adult. Before the adopted child reaches adulthood, "many parents try to persuade themselves that adoption has been best for their children and have difficulty considering any other possibilities" (2004, p12). Whilst their children are minors, birth parents often assume a self-protective mode and any thoughts of searching are deferred. Also,

The Invisible Men of Adoption

under most jurisdictions, any outreach made by a birth parent to their pre-adult child must by law be directed through the adoptive parents. This is a scenario, in situations where birth and adoptive parents are not in regular contact, that most birth parents avoid, out of consideration for the child, as well as, perhaps, their own emotional fragility.

When both parties are adults, other factors come into consideration. As the child reaches adulthood, the birth parents are typically in the mid-span of their years, often a time when subsequent children they have parented are on the cusp of becoming or have become adults, so consolidating their own identities. This is also a time when parents perhaps contemplate their lives to date. Sometimes, memories of the past may be resurrected by the arrival of grandchildren. Mid-life may be when a birth parent feels that they are ready to search, not only for their authentic self, but also for the now adult child whom they lost through adoption. Also, it may coincide with the time when birth parents are aware that the child they lost is legally now able to initiate the search for their antecedents. Irrespective of who initiates the search, the sought reunion is between two adults, each in a position to take responsibility for their own actions and decisions.

A self-aware birth parent may initiate personal mending as preparation for the possibility of being 'found' by his adult child, albeit as a postponed activity. As noted by Cicchini (1993), it may be years, even decades after the event, that birth fathers allow themselves to ponder, as 'men', the full consequences of the actions they took, in many cases, when they were adolescents. This may be the first time the father has faced the hurt he caused the mother, and by association, the child she carried through pregnancy, to lose to an adoption. This may be when he finally admits to and confronts his own pain, the time when he permits his submerged feelings about the losses to surface. These feelings may include a postponed reaction to the grief he perhaps suppressed at the time of the adoption. In parallel with or as a result of dealing with his issues, the birth father may feel that he now wants to reach out to the other members of the family of origin. However, he may hold back because of either an unwillingness to intrude upon the lives of the adult child and the birth mother, or fears about the reception he might receive.

There are sound reasons for the delay of a birth father's acknowledgment of the impact of adoption upon himself. Because a birth father does not carry a child for nine months and establish in-utero bonding and because he is often not present at the birth of his child, it may be easier for him to deceive himself that the loss of his child has had little impact on his sense of self. This does not mean that a father ceases to have any regard for his child after the adoption. There is evidence that birth fathers think "frequently" or "constantly" about their child (Cicchini, 1993, p8), whilst at the same time choosing to do nothing about their concerns, until a catalyst for action occurs. For a birth mother, the loss of her child is likely to be an ever-present factor in her life. Because of the severing of the biological bond she forged with her unborn baby, a birth mother is perhaps more likely to have a high degree of continuing awareness of the impact of being separated from her child. However, for birth fathers, in part because of the absence of the biological in-utero linkage, there may be a postponed awareness of the impact of parent–child separation on their lives.

When a birth father does decide to confront his adoption experience, he may find that he has significant barriers to overcome, a legacy of both the dual focus of his guilt and the time he has buried his feelings. Birth fathers may bury their guilt for many years, because it feels too confronting to expose their selves to themselves, let alone others. As noted by Jones, the load may be so great that, even within an apparently safe environment, some birth fathers elect to stay 'closed' – "Many [birth mothers married to the birth father] believed that the birthfathers would have preferred to remain in permanent denial rather than risk confrontations with their long-buried emotions" (1993, pp238–239).

The Invisible Men of Adoption

Compounded guilt, centred on mother <u>and</u> child, may be the anxiety that either impels a birth father to act out of a sense of remorse or drives him to seek refuge within himself. There is another, social factor. A birth father may have absorbed society's evolved attitudes to fatherhood. Forty and more years ago, according to Clapton, "societal expectations of fathers – during pregnancy and childbirth, of their involvement in childcare and domestic tasks – were less" (2003, p48). The man who was not there for his child may, against today's expectation of more involved parenting, feel guilty about his past neglect. Thus, for a birth father, guilt may provide either the incentive or an impediment to searching and to healing. A birth father's guilt may be either too much to bear or too much to bare. In the latter circumstance, birth fathers opt to internalise their pain. They may take no action to deal with their past, and so be in a position to assist the birth mother and the now adult child with their recoveries. It is possible that these men have little or no appreciation of the withheld opportunities to help the other members of the family of origin to heal. This insight is likely to arise only after a birth father has dealt with his own adoption issues. The realisation that effort is required may dawn slowly, as occurred in my case. Progress can be faltering, because the perceived risks appear to outweigh the potential benefits of exposure. If he is contacted by his (adult) adopted child or the birth mother, the birth father may be prodded into action.

Because some men (including birth fathers) find it difficult to process their feelings, even when in their forties, fifties and sixties, they may prefer to restrict their search to seeking information about their now adult child, as well as perhaps the birth mother. For these men, knowing that the persons about whose welfare they care are alive, may be enough. In other words, they have satisfied the desire to know and this may be the degree to which they are prepared to search. To make contact and face the probability of having to confront not only their own feelings but the emotions of those persons from whom they were separated before or at the time of the adoption may be too difficult for some men to tackle. This scenario could account for the reported phenomenon of men, adopted persons and birth fathers alike, being well represented in post-adoption support organisations' enquiry statistics but under-represented in situations that involve interpersonal communication, such as support groups, conferences, seminars and reunions.

The benefits of being open

I believe that those men who sate their curiosity and proceed no further let down themselves and those from whom they were separated. In my opinion, you display generosity not only to yourself but also to your child and his or her birth mother if you reach out and initiate contact, or if approached first, you accept the overture. By making yourself available, you convey to others that you value them as persons. The alternative of invisibility may suggest that you are selfish and uncaring, a perpetuation of the traditional stereotype of the birth father.

As a birth father, you may believe that determining that your child and the birth mother are alive is a significant act, one that appeases your concerns. In itself, this may be psychologically healthy, but it does not benefit the subjects of your curiosity, for they are unlikely to be aware of your personal quest for solace. It is through a willingness to participate in reunion that a birth father displays not only charity and unselfishness, but also that he truly cares about the persons from whom he was separated by the adoption. By reaching out, the birth father presents himself to the birth mother and his adult child. Each can then consider his offer and avail themselves of the opportunity to include him in their respective lives.

For those birth fathers who remain closed, evidence suggests that it is unhealthy, physically and psychologically to live under duress. Suppressing a guilty secret and remaining ever-vigilant to ensure that it is never released is stressful. I maintain that you cannot live a full life, one celebrated by personal well-

The Invisible Men of Adoption

being and an openness with others, if there is a part of yourself that you are afraid to reveal. Not only do you constrain yourself, but also you prevent others from knowing your authentic self. It is my experience that family, friends and strangers appreciate your transparency. In addition, they do not fulfil the fears that you may have about being judged harshly by them for your past indiscretions. In other words, the community may be more understanding than you, perhaps mired in guilt, are prepared to contemplate. This alone, apart from the important health considerations, makes disclosure of your adoption experience beneficial.

According to Jennifer Newbould, manager of ARCS in Western Australia (personal communication, 2004), birth fathers who initiate outreach often proceed slowly – a step at a time, punctuated by lengthy pauses. Few seek counselling, but those who do (and these are birth fathers who rarely have spoken of their adoption experience or their feelings) often find the unburdening very therapeutic. In the 2008 survey conducted by Passmore and Coles, those birth fathers who had undertaken counselling generally reported that they found the service to be "moderately" or "extremely helpful." One birth father added that the counsellor was "very skilled."

Newbould concludes that those birth fathers who search display great patience and seem not to have high expectations. In my opinion, this may be a manifestation of the guilt that birth fathers can retain – a conflict between the personal need to salve their consciences and a reluctance to remind themselves of the hurt they caused mother and child. Advance, then pause (or even retreat) may seem a safe option. Being found is perhaps a more comfortable alternative and here, according to Newbould, more and more adopted people are today acknowledging that they have birth fathers as well as birth mothers.

There may be those birth fathers who, aware of their status, resist facing their adoption issues, because they believe that the activity will disrupt their lives. I contend that their equilibrium was disturbed by the original separation. It is by addressing the impact of the parting that birth fathers incorporate their adoption experience into their lives and so achieve progress.

There are other birth fathers who blame the birth mother for the loss of their child. These are the men who perhaps refuse to accept that they too played a role in the events that led to the adoption. In some cases this censure may represent the projection of a birth father's guilt. I maintain that this stance is a selfish one, which is often at odds with the events that took place.

For those men who are surprised many years later to be told that they fathered a child, the news presents an opportunity to welcome a new member into their extended family. The degree to which the birth father accepts his new-found status will depend much upon how he views himself. If he is open to exploring possibilities, this incorporation may be smooth. For other more wary, closed men, this information may be perceived as a threat.

If the claim of paternity from the searching child (now an adult) is well-founded, then a birth father might well pause to consider that his son or daughter has reached out to him, put aside his shock and any apprehensions and honour the initiative taken. Reunion, whether activated by yourself or the other person from whom you were separated prior to or at the time of the adoption, presents an opportunity for reconciliation. If the reunion is perceived to be likely to change the lives of the participants, this is an expected response. In the case of father and child, the meeting presents the first opportunity to experience mirroring (seeing yourself in the other person), allowing issues embracing identity, loss and grief to surface.

Other birth fathers who have no information about their child on which to base a search, may feel relieved to be approached. When Florence Fisher contacts her birth father after a separation of more than four decades, his spontaneous response is "This is the most wonderful moment of my life!" (Fisher, 1973, p256). He explains: "All these years, ... I used to look at children in the street and think, somewhere I have a daughter. Wherever you were, I didn't know who you were, but I always loved you" (Fisher, 1973, p257). Florence Fisher is an example (some would

The Invisible Men of Adoption

say an inspiration) to those people who encounter difficulties when they search for members of their birth family. Despite facing apparently insuperable barriers in gaining access to information, she refused to give up and eventually found an avenue to her birth father. She personifies the adage that 'where there's a will, there's a way'.

Admitting to fathering a child is not the end of the world. Rather, you may find, as I did, that it represents the launching of a fulfilling phase of your life. You may feel liberated, relieved that the truth is out, that you no longer have to carry the burden of a secret about your past. You may find that you are capable (at last!) of enjoying much of what life has to offer. You will perhaps discover, as a result of being more open, that the breadth and depth of your friendships increase. Ultimately, of course, you are better prepared to appreciate reunion with the persons from whom you were separated by the adoption, and so give of yourself for their (and your) benefit.

Stromberg comments that to improve how they are perceived by the community, "Birth fathers need ... to portray themselves not as villains, but deserving members of society and of the adoption system. This can be done through the telling of life stories by birth fathers via the media and literature" (2002, p83). Stromberg then makes a telling point – "it is much easier for society to lay blame on a faceless institution rather than an individual and therefore birth fathers ... need to promote an image that contrasts with the traditional image portrayed by society. Birth fathers could then be viewed from a different paradigm" (*ibid*). I urge all birth fathers to rise to this challenge.

The Invisible Men of Adoption

The Invisible Men of Adoption

Duo

CHAPTER 6

Birth parents who remain mum

"It's not denial. I'm just selective about the reality I accept." — Bill Watterson

There are moments in the lives of many of us when we, despite the best intentions, defer taking action. Sometimes, we halt because we wish to contemplate the possible consequences for our selves and the potential impact on others. Perhaps, we are apprehensive about the unknown, wary of stepping beyond familiar territory. Maybe we lack the courage or the support of others to take those first steps, so we prevaricate. In this circumstance, inaction's helpmates, secrecy and denial might beckon.

Traditionally, adoption literature on secrecy and denial has focussed on adoptive families, for example Passmore *et al* (2007). They surveyed 144 adopted persons and their findings included: "Adoptees who had experienced greater secrecy within their adoptive families felt less emotionally close to their adoptive parents, perceived their adoptive parents as less caring and more controlling, and experienced greater loneliness within the family context." Passmore *et al* also noted that lies, secrecy and misinformation perpetrated by adoptive parents can have consequences for adopted persons in critical aspects of their lives, such as: "(a) identity, search and reunion experiences; (b) [the] relationship with their adoptive parents, and (c) relationships with other people." Overall, "By making adoption a taboo topic, some adoptive parents denied their children information about their backgrounds. Such secrecy also led some adoptees to subsequently keep their own search and/or reunion a secret from their adoptive parents."

By contrast, there have been few formal studies about secrecy and denial, as practised by birth parents. However, from those birth parents who have shared their experiences, it is known anecdotally that after the adoption, many became discreet about their 'status'. Some also have denied the impact of the loss of their child, and in some cases, the loss of a significant relationship with the other parent.

Often, birth parents' release from these inhibitors has been compromised, particularly in the recorded instances of their being hoodwinked by what seemed at the time to be altruistic assurances, which proved to be hollow. It is on record that many birth mothers were promised by family members and social workers that 'the child is going to a secure family environment, which you cannot provide' and 'your child is a gift to a couple who cannot have children of their own'. Physical abuse has occurred in some adoptive families. Adoptive parents have divorced; others conceived children of their own after the adoption.

Then there were the placatory claims of 'you have done the right thing for the child and yourself', 'you will forget that this ever happened', 'soon enough, you will put this behind you' and the almost universal 'you will be able to get on with your life'. Against the background of such expressions of certainty, it is little wonder that so many birth mothers felt cheated when these declarations turned out to be misguided. There is an argument that what birth mothers were told was a reflection of the social milieu of the time and that on this basis the promises are acceptable. I reject this benign interpretation. The advice, frequently from the lips of so-called professionals was grounded not in evidence, but in ignorance and misjudgement.

There were also people who recklessly promised birth mothers permanent concealment. Against a background of perpetually evolving social attitudes, it was inevitable that such an assertion would be exposed for its fiction. Women who accepted the vow that the secret of their pregnancy and the resultant adopted child would never be revealed have been forced to confront the consequences of their pain and their shame later in life. "These women may feel enormous anger at having been subsequently contacted and this can interfere with them coming to terms with changing times and changed attitudes. As well as disenfranchising themselves by internalising the unresolved pain, they also disenfranchise their adopted daughter or son, more so when they will not allow any information about [the adopted person's birth] father, family relationships, health, or the beginning of the child's identity and story" (Marshall, 1999, p7).

In VANISH Incorporated (2004), 'Joy and Friends (Natural Mothers)' reflect on secrecy in adoption. They note: "From the moment most women discovered they were pregnant, secrecy entered their lives forever." They outline the manifestations – the hiding away in disgrace to protect the family from shame, avoiding the anger and disappointment of parents by moving interstate, returning to families and living within a network of lies to explain their recent absence, the self-deception thought necessary to maintain the acceptance of friends and extended family, and withholding the knowledge of the out-of-wedlock pregnancy so that the opportunity for subsequent marriage was not jeopardised.

Because many birth mothers kept silent, it was assumed that they had actually forgotten the loss of their child and carried on with their lives, as if the adoption had never occurred. What was actually a suppressed persona was construed by the wider community to be gravitas allied with maturity. That birth mothers kept their son or daughter a secret (an illegitimate child was socially unacceptable, *ie* a bastard, in the language of the times) and buried their feelings, perpetuated the illusion that these women bore no residual issues from the loss of their child. In this surreal setting, it is little wonder that the preservation of secrets behind a wall of denial was seen by birth mothers to be socially sanctioned.

The Invisible Men of Adoption

As noted by Hartman, "It was felt that the stigmatized birth mother, who had been guilty of sexual misconduct, was protected by denial and secrecy ... As soon as she signed the relinquishment papers, she ceased to exist. She not only carried a secret, but *was* a secret" (1993, pp87–88) [emphasis in the reference]. Gediman and Brown pursue the same point, noting that denial "... intensifies the birthparents' poor self image, by reinforcing the idea that what they have done is so heinous that it must forever be concealed" (1991, p14). A birth mother may also feel that she is a failure (after all, how can you be a mother and give up a baby?), if she is unable to resolve the grief associated with the loss of her child. She may bury her misgivings, which reinforces the denial. She may carry her burden silently for years. She may even take her shameful secret to the grave.

Portuesi notes: "Denial becomes survival for most birth mothers. Frequently the ability to love or trust again is arrested. The psychological trauma may also cause amnesia around certain aspects of the experience .... when the feelings around loss are arrested, so are other feelings like anger, joy and happiness ... Life becomes muted" (2000, pp5–6). Concludes Portuesi: "The relinquishment of a child for adoption permeates all aspects of a birth mother's life" (p5). In a social environment where they felt they had few choices, the "mother-to-be often had to 'hide' as a way to safeguard her secret from friends and family" (*ibid*). Van Keppel *et al* write: "A ... factor which contributes to interpersonal difficulties is that for many, the relinquishment remains a secret – a secret they have typically kept because their family and friends may reject them were they to know. The continued support of family is often conditional on the birth mother maintaining her secret. Many have not told their husbands and other significant family members [including children]" and "... the secret many birth mothers carry has contributed to persistent feelings of isolation, alienation and unworthiness" (1987, p5). Often, a birth mother's feelings about the adoption are complicated by two factors, *viz* the loss of her child is concurrently a source of joy for the adoptive parents and there is no 'body' to associate with her grief, for the child may appear in person as an adult, asking to be re-incorporated into her life.

Birth fathers too experience a loss, similar in many aspects to that of birth mothers. Gary Clapton, writing as G Colvin in *A Cache of Feelings Buried in a Time Capsule* (1996) on the Internet, reflects on the 25 years between becoming a birth father and being found by his daughter, Jane: "... I ask myself why I did not wonder about my daughter's welfare and development in the years she was growing up? ... My daughter's adoption had little or no bearing on my life. Or so I used to think" and "[the signing of the papers] is a significant event – the significance of which is somehow buried deep underground yet still capable of causing explosions." He concludes his self-analysis: "I ask myself this: if my daughter had not got in touch with me would I have carried on believing that I first became a father just six years ago with the birth of my eldest son?" The language here is of a birth father who was in denial for a quarter of a century.

The majority of the thirty men in Cicchini's study report difficulties telling others about the relinquishment of their child. One man offered: "Most situations you have regrets about, you have trouble telling others about" (1993, p8). Another birth father was more specific: "I've lived with the knowledge that my child is out there somewhere but have pretended to the world he doesn't exist" (Cicchini, 1993, p13). Riedel, writing in Mason (1995) observes: "Birthfathers often keep their fatherhood a secret out of shame. Not speaking about the experience shuts down the grief process in its early stages and negatively impacts (*sic*) the development of trust, identity, intimacy, sexuality and self-esteem. A father may avoid events that remind him of the original wound, or he may deny the birthfather experience altogether by saying ... 'I never saw the child so it doesn't really exist' " (pp264–265).

According to Gediman and Brown, those birth fathers who have kept their fatherhood a secret, particularly from their wives and children, "are presented with the same dilemma that found birthmothers face: to tell or not to tell" (1991, p176). They go on

The Invisible Men of Adoption

to write of adopted persons who "presented themselves to birthfathers who proved unable or unwilling to tell their wives and families about the adoptee's existence. This usually is labeled 'protecting his family' and amounts to a hello–goodbye contact ..." (pp176–177).

There are inherent risks when birth parents withhold information from immediate family. A deferred revelation ('I will tell them someday ... when the time is right') has the potential to become a time bomb. The secret may be exposed to family members anyway, perhaps inadvertently by another person, leaving a legacy of distrust, loss of faith and perhaps anger towards the person who has held the secret close. For relatives of birth parents who have taken the secret of their parenthood to the grave, the information, when exposed, perhaps by the searching adult adopted person, can have a devastating effect on the family of the deceased.

According to Hartman, keeping a secret from family and friends not only cuts off a birth parent from comfort and support, but also makes them vulnerable to exposure and shame (1993, p93). For birth mothers and birth fathers alike, shame is a harsh consequence of having given their child a 'better home'. This is a legacy they are unlikely to have anticipated, when given the 'usual assurances' at the time of the adoption.

There are other effects that result from denial and keeping secrets. Imber-Black notes that a secret preserved by one individual "often erodes self-esteem and one's capacity to trust other people's responses, because the secret-keeper often feels 'If others really knew, they would dislike me, disrespect me, hate me, etc' ..." Sometimes, the "secret becomes denied, repressed, and a secret even from oneself" (1993, p21).

Devoting unproductive energy to maintaining a secret has a negative effect on relationships between a birth parent (or an adopted person) and other people. Transparency and a willingness to take risks, to explore, to live life to the full, are compromised by the felt necessity to remain closed, to keep the shameful part of oneself buried.

The Invisible Men of Adoption

From many perspectives, denial and secrecy are counter-productive. They block the growth of the very persons who hold and internalise the unnecessary burden. Like a dead weight, they impede progress. Not only is the keeper of the secret disadvantaged, but also the person from whom the secret is withheld. Being made privy to the information may assist the resolution of their personal issues. The keeper of the information has no right to exercise control over the person who is the subject of the information. In the case of excluded birth parents, this may be an unpleasant reminder of how they felt when the adoption was arranged.

CHAPTER 7

Guilt throwers and guilt catchers

"In nature there are neither rewards nor punishments - there are consequences." — Robert Green Ingersoll

In an audio series called *The Psychology of Achievement*, Brian Tracy speaks of 'guilt throwers and guilt catchers', *ie* people who are adept at using guilt to control others and those who are vulnerable, because of conditioning, to manipulation. I see a connection with adoption.

Adopted persons and birth parents have spoken of carrying residual guilt, related to the separation of the members of the family of origin. Some adopted persons have reported that they believe their arrival caused the separation of the birth parents. Birth mothers may internalise their guilt, a reaction associated with becoming pregnant and 'allowing' the infant to be adopted. For some birth fathers, their guilt can centre on having let the birth mother down, so leaving her with little option but to place the child for adoption.

Later, to integrate the loss and grief resulting from the initial separation into their lives, adopted persons and birth parents may choose to devote energy to trying to understand the source and the impact of their guilt. Frequently this task is not easy and to be reminded of their discomfort by guilt throwers can undermine, or at best retard personal healing. People with adoption experiences who have not yet initiated personal healing are particularly vulnerable to catching projected guilt.

The Invisible Men of Adoption

The most damaging manipulation can occur within post-adoption relationships. Through perhaps a lack of understanding or jealousy, partners sometimes belittle the adoption experience of a birth parent or an adopted person. Often with a non-adoption background, these people may employ tactics that question the decisions that resulted in the adoption. For a birth parent in particular, the guilt associated with the original separation may resurface and generate a fresh bout of emotional turmoil. Sometimes the guilt thrower will insist that their partner have nothing to do with the other members of their birth family, so that if a birth parent or an adopted person chooses to pursue or to maintain contact, they do so covertly, without the blessing of the partner. Such a situation is not conducive to the good health of one or other of the relationships. For example, a birth mother may feel guilty if she goes behind her husband's back and allows contact with the birth father or her now adult child. Equally, guilt may be her reaction if she does not make herself available to an outreach from her child.

In the case of some birth mothers, the guilt may be aggravated by the fear of discovery, that a disapproving husband will unearth any search or reunion initiatives. For a woman in this situation, inaction may represent a 'survival' strategy. The preservation of the marriage, irrespective of the quality of the relationship between husband and wife, may be her paramount consideration, because the union fulfils her basic needs. In this unfortunate circumstance, potentially the psychological health of the repressed birth parent is at risk. The opportunities to satisfy the higher human needs of belonging, self-esteem and self-actualisation can be compromised.

Some guilt throwers ask that an adopted person or a birth parent dismiss their adoption experience altogether. For those who previously have practised denial as a means of protection, this request that they regress can create distress and cause them to feel guilty about (again) excluding members of their birth family.

Typically, birth parents and adopted persons do not wish their outreach initiatives to harm relationships within the adoptive family. Sometimes, though, because of perceived adoptive parent sensitivities, members of the birth family defer searching. Often, their reservations about the reactions of the adoptive parents prove to be unfounded. There are instances, though, of adoptive parents making it known that they view search and reunion as a censure of their parenting skills. The spectre of outreach, whether initiated by the adult adopted person or the birth parent, may also, for the adoptive parents, resurrect their infertility issues and the reality that the child they have raised cannot replace the children that were never born to them.

Members of the family of origin are best served by not becoming embroiled in any guilt projected by the adoptive parents. The adoptive mother and the adoptive father alone bear the responsibility for their actions and reactions. The adult adopted child and the birth parents remain bystanders.

Brian Tracy writes about guilt throwers and guilt catchers in his book *Maximum Achievement*, which expands on the material covered in the audio material. For guilt catchers, he has this advice: "Each time anyone says or does anything to make you feel guilty, and you acquiesce to their demands, you reinforce the guilty feeling and make it easier for people to manipulate you in the future. You should have a decent respect for the feelings and needs of others, but this doesn't mean you should sacrifice your emotional integrity to them" (1995, p225). Continuing, Tracy suggests two strategies – silence and assertiveness. To me, the first, in which the catcher is encouraged to stonewall and refuse to respond, is countering one form of manipulation with another, *viz* passive control. Further, the muteness of the catcher may be misconstrued by the thrower as either capitulation or withdrawal from the relationship. The alternative method involves engaging the guilt thrower. Tracy writes: "When the other person attempts to manipulate you using guilt, you respond by saying, 'Are you trying to make me feel guilty?' You ask this question in a low-keyed nonthreatening way, even with a tone of genuine wonder and curiosity, as if you're amazed at such a possibility" (1995, p226). As this approach encourages dialogue, it offers more possibilities for a productive outcome.

The impact on relationships of guilt throwing and catching can be likened to a game of social tennis. If one player belts serves and ground strokes, which the other is unable to return, the match is certain to be short, and for the vanquished, disheartening. A match in which equally talented players show respect for each other is likely to be rewarding for both people. Relationship-wise, the absence of guilt throwers and catchers makes for bountiful matches.

CHAPTER 8

The role of control

"I cannot always control what goes on outside. But I can always control what goes on inside." – Wayne Dyer

A pervasive issue for those with adoption experiences is an accompanying feeling of helplessness. Disempowerment and disenfranchisement are but two outcomes reported by those who were not in control of critical, life-changing decisions.

This chapter explores the impact of locus of control on those whose lives have been affected by adoption. The good news is that with awareness, we have the personal capacity to process our experiences and bring their meaning and impact back within our command.

Control and well-being – the theory

The literature on personal development contains many allusions to the positive correlation between the well-being of an individual and the degree of influence they are able to exert over their life. That we can assert our independent will is possible because of the unique human endowment of self-awareness, which is accompanied by an ability to exercise, between stimulus and response, the freedom of choice. Covey (1990) concludes that the response we choose is an indication of the degree to which we are prepared to be responsible for our lives. He describes proactive people, those whose behaviour is a function of the decisions they have made: "They do not blame circumstances, conditions, or conditioning for their behaviour. Their behaviour is a product of their own conscious choice" (p71). However, he goes on, "if our lives are a function of conditioning and conditions, it is because we have, by conscious decision or by default, chosen to empower those things to control us. In making such a choice we become reactive" (*ibid*). Reactive people allow other people and circumstances to control them, whereas proactive people, although aware of external influences, make a conscious effort to factor these stimuli into their responses.

Covey then explores the notion of where we focus our energy and time. Those people who are reactive, *ie* are acted upon, concentrate their efforts on what he calls the Circle of Concern, which embraces blaming and feelings of victimisation, caused by events over which they feel they have no control. This is an inward looking, contracting circle. Those people who are proactive display initiative and take responsibility for their lives. Theirs is an outward looking, expanding Circle of Influence.

Whilst we are free to determine our actions, this does not mean that we get to choose the consequences of our actions. Also, sometimes these consequences are not what we envisaged when we took the action. If we had the ability to reconsider the action that had led to an undesired outcome, we would proceed differently. The key here is to acknowledge the mistake and learn from it.

In an ideal world, we would choose to be in charge of our lives at all times. However, there are circumstances, in which our conditioning, learned from our upbringing and the social environment we inhabit, sometimes inhibits our ability to act proactively. We feel we are prevented from exercising control over key facets of our lives. The result is stress, not a sense of well-being.

The Invisible Men of Adoption

Control and adoption – the practice

Adoption is an experience in which the issue of control features significantly. For most birth parents, if they had exercised their first choice, the result would not have been an adoption! Adoption then is often a reactive choice, contrary to the Covey ideal of dominant, proactive Circle of Influence deliberations.

Birth parents were, at the time their child was conceived and decisions required about their collective futures, typically young and immature. Perhaps, at this age, they had not yet acquired the life skills and the confidence to make proactive decisions. Given this circumstance, they have, influenced by their upbringing, allowed others to make life-changing decisions on their behalf, whilst not necessarily convinced that they were doing the right thing, but feeling powerless to oppose the proposed actions. The feeling of helplessness and sense of wrongness experienced by birth mothers in particular are extensively documented in the literature. These are the reactions of women who have the first-hand experience of control being wrested from them. Of the consequences, Verrier (1993) has this to say:

> "Because they gave up a child, many birthmothers consider themselves bad mothers, undeserving of having another child or unable to be good mothers to their other children. This belief often persists, regardless of their circumstances at the time of giving birth or the coercive tactics used to get them to feel guilty for wanting to keep their babies. Whether a birthmother gave up her baby because she realized she could not care properly for him or because others convinced her of this, she must understand she did what she was capable of doing at the time. We could live lives of regret if we were to dwell on the mistakes we have made in our lives. But regret is one of those useless occupiers of our time and energy which gain us nothing. A birthmother cannot change what happened, but she can forgive herself for her decision or let go of the guilt if she really had no control over that decision" (p183).

The Invisible Men of Adoption

To regain the 'power within', Verrier advocates the challenging of old belief systems, including the need for approval, which may have guided previous actions, embracing, for example, the reluctance of a birth mother to tell her parents that she was pregnant. She goes on: "Mistakes are risks taken that didn't work out ... Mistakes give us another way of gaining information. As children, we may have feared that our parent wouldn't approve of us if we made mistakes. That may or may not have been a true evaluation of the situation. Now, however, we need to approve of ourselves, so we can forgive ourselves our mistakes and just accept the lesson they teach us" (1993, p194).

Robinson (2002) provides some practical advice on how this outcome can be achieved. Describing the post-adoption grief counselling service offered at that time to the clients of the Association Representing Mothers Separated from their Children by Adoption (ARMS) in South Australia, she first recognises that grief is a healthy response to the adoption experience. She then outlines the methodology, which, after acknowledging the enormity and complexity of the loss of a child to adoption and the powerlessness experienced by the mothers at the time of separation, counsels the client to increased feelings of self-worth and empowerment. This is facilitated by encouraging the mothers to re-examine the values and beliefs they acquired during childhood and adolescence, as well as the attitudes to which they were subjected when they were pregnant and the influences critical to the decision to adopt. The continuing impact of the loss of the child on the mothers' lives is also discussed. As Robinson explains, "The principal function of the counselling is to allow the suppressed grief to surface and be experienced in a constructive manner that is accepted and understood by the mother. Secondly, the counselling helps the mother to make the links and connections between her life events and the values, beliefs and motives that give them meaning. For many mothers, it is the first time that certain patterns have become apparent. This often leads to empowering moments of clarity and acceptance, and to a reduction in feelings of guilt and shame" (2002, p61).

South Australian mothers have been the beneficiaries of this service. For the many birth parents, mothers and fathers alike, who do not have access to post-adoption grief counselling, all is not lost. The alternative, taking a proactive, responsible approach, is self-help, *ie* conducting a personal analysis of the actions and reactions that comprise an individual's adoption experience. This is an activity controlled by the participant and one that has the potential to increase personal understanding and well-being.

Those closest to the individual birth parents have a critical role to play in assisting them to process their adoption experiences. In most cases, the most influential person is the husband or wife of the birth parent. The attitude of the spouse to the initial revelation of the birth mother's (or birth father's) role in the conception and adoption of another child is important. If the spouse demonstrates understanding and acceptance, then this augurs well for the birth parent and the addressing of their grief. If however, the spouse displays disapproval of their partner's past and inhibits, or worse, prohibits further discussion about the matter and the impact of the loss of the child, then subsequent healing will be very difficult for the birth parent. In this latter undesirable situation, the spouse is imposing their narrow-mindedness on the birth parent, cementing the grief and reinforcing the shame experienced by those who have lost children through adoption. The spouse may blame the other birth parent for damaging the person they came to marry. Where the birth mother has embarked on another close relationship (which culminates in marriage) soon after losing her child, she may be particularly vulnerable. If her husband makes it clear that he prefers she keep her past hidden from personal and public exposure, then his hold over her may be strong. Indeed, he may tell her that not only has he rescued her from emotional turmoil, but also he has provided her with the chance to become respectable. In such circumstances, operating from within her Circle of Concern may seem safer for the birth mother wife.

The Invisible Men of Adoption

If the birth parent, wanting resolution of personal issues resulting from the loss of their child, is unable to secure the support of the spouse, their seeking support elsewhere may be unwelcome, with possible negative consequences for the marriage. Some birth parents may choose to buck the imposed control anyway by taking the initiative, hoping that their improved well-being will become obvious to their spouse.

Obviously, openness within the marriage is the key to a birth parent's healing. If husband and wife communicate well on a spectrum of levels and topics, then neither partner is likely to exert control over the other, whether overt or covert, and dialogues about the impact of the loss of a child to adoption will occur in an atmosphere of mutual respect and tolerance. Threats to personal equilibrium, with the potential to test the relationship between husband and wife, could arise if the birth parent fulfils the opportunity to unearth their buried pain. A more palpable threat may be the return of the other birth parent or the lost child – the spouse may feel jealous or temporarily excluded, as their birth parent partner explores the meaning of these renewed relationships and tries to incorporate them into their life. Here again, the support and understanding of the spouse plays a key role.

For adopted persons, control is fundamental. They had no say about being separated from their birth mother. Control, as a central issue in their lives, has its source in the fear that, feeling they have been abandoned at birth, they may be given up a second time. If they allow somebody to control their lives again, the fate that befell them the first time could recur. Their reaction to this fear may be a desperate need to be in control of themselves and their environment at all times, which may include manipulating other people. Other adopted persons deliberately diminish the risk of being abandoned by becoming the compliant child, thereby avoiding the possibility of their not being considered good enough to keep. These adopted persons have, in effect, handed control of their behaviour to the adoptive parents.

The Invisible Men of Adoption

The penchant for control exerted by adopted persons may, because of childhood conditioning, continue into adulthood. The search for the birth parents may become particularly significant, as explained by Brodzinsky *et al* (1993):

> "The activated search provides an important psychological function for some people: it allows them to gain control over forces over which they previously had no control. Many adoptees complain about feeling subject to the vicissitudes of a capricious fate – that they were put up for adoption in the first place, adopted by a particular family, denied information about their past. Searching can bring the locus of control from 'out there' to 'inside' themselves. It allows the adoptee to experience the self as capable of acting rather than being acted upon – a major factor in establishing a healthier identity" (p142).

Sarah Saffian is one adopted person who relates to these observations. As the subject of the search by her birth parents, she bristles: "I resent ... having the control of knowledge taken away from me ... I had planned on setting out to find you when I was ready" (1998, p25).

Searching, whether by an adopted person or a birth parent, is a reaching out, initiated by one person, without the other person being at first aware of the activity. For the initiator, it often involves risks, because, paradoxically, by taking control, it opens the possibility of creating a chain of events that threatens to cascade out of control, emotionally. The rebuttal of a searcher's approach, perhaps culminating, in the case of New Zealand and several Australian states with the imposition of a veto is, however, a self-centred action taken by a person intent on holding control. It is risk averse and manipulates the lives of other persons, the actual (or potential) searchers, whether they be adopted persons or birth parents. A refusal to sanction contact is possibly, in the case of adopted persons, imposed punitively, as a response to the perception that they 'owe nothing' to the persons who gave them up in the first instance.

The Invisible Men of Adoption

Birth parents who search for their children have chosen to act from within their Circle of Influence. This is so also for adopted person searchers who choose to proceed. Those adult adopted persons, often well represented at support groups, who express ambivalence about commencing a search, for fear that they will upset their adoptive parents and be perceived as betraying the people who raised them, are relinquishing control to those parents and in some instances, the memory of them. Some adopted persons, facing the risk of hurting the adoptive parents, decide never to tell them about the search. Again the covert constraining influence of the adoptive parents is present.

Overt control may be exerted by adoptive parents. On record are those who have colluded with social workers or acted independently to concoct a story that the birth parents do not exist – they died together in a car accident, thus rendering a search for them pointless. Adoptive parents who choose never to tell their children that they are adopted, are exhibiting complete domination. Adoptive parents who defer telling their child that they are adopted, using the excuse that the recipients are not yet ready to hear the news, may be exercising a form of control, because of an unwillingness to face their own parenting issues. Some adoptive parents, whilst acknowledging the status of their children and apparently sanctioning contact with the birth parents, are actually lukewarm about the possibility of it occurring. For example, a 'we don't mind if you want to find your birth parents' does not carry the same message of support as the empowering 'we encourage you to explore your heritage'. When 23-year-old Sarah Saffian's birth mother contacts her unexpectedly, the adoptive mother's response is: "Why couldn't she have contacted us instead, so at least we could have acted as an intermediary?" (Saffian, 1998, p12). Here is a parent who acts in an overly protective manner towards the child she has raised, forgetting that her daughter is an adult who is capable of making her own choices, including that of not living at home. It is unlikely that in a non-adoptive setting an enquirer would seek permission to contact another adult via his or her parents.

The Invisible Men of Adoption

For other adoptive parents, informed by social workers that the right of the birth parents to play a role in the adopted child's life was extinguished by the adoption order, there is a perceived certainty that the child belongs to them, without any threat of intervention. Such an assertion made at the time of the adoption was reckless, because it takes no account of probable future changes in social attitudes and legislation. An adopted person raised in this environment is likely to feel uncomfortable about exploring their origins, particularly in the extreme situation where the adoptive parents make it abundantly clear that they resent any approach by the birth parents. This circumstance may result in the adopted person placing a veto, to display loyalty to and placate the adoptive parents. The veto hampers attempts by the birth parents either to be privy to information about or to locate the adopted person. Bowing to the fears of the adoptive parents is putting their needs first. The adopted person is disempowered; they are responding to external controls. Saffian exemplifies such a reaction. Wondering if meeting her birth parents will bring her a sense of peace, she writes: "I suppose that would depend on my adoptive parents' reaction to the reunion: if they acted threatened and detached, I would feel guilty; if they were supportive and interested, I would feel whole" (1998, p165). The alternative viewpoint is conveyed by another adopted person in Blau (1993): "My past is part of me, and no one has the right to rob me of a reunion because of their insecurities" (p26).

Control then, has a profound effect on people whose lives are affected by adoption. The adoption itself is an experience over which the principal participants often had little or no influence. Post-adoption responses, however, are governed by the degree to which participants in the adoption are prepared to allow their proactive Circle of Influence to reign over a reactive Circle of Concern. Here, the choice whether or not to seek to understand and to heal is ours.

CHAPTER 9

The incentive to search

"All glory comes from daring to begin." — Eugene Ware

Introduction

Without an adoption in the first instance and the consequent loss, there would be no need for search and reunion. The search is a natural response by adopted persons and birth parents; it is typically an attempt to redress the loss caused by adoption. The loss, manifested as a physical separation, is tangible. A person is missing. The psychological aspects of loss, coupled with the deprivation of heritage (for an adopted person) and the passing on of the genetic line (for the birth parents) are deeper and more difficult to identify and resolve.

Adopted persons and birth parents have every right to view the separation of parent and child, the result of the practice of adoption, as a disempowering event. It is true of adopted persons that, as infants, they were not in a position to exercise any control over what was happening to them. Decisions were made on their behalf, ostensibly in their best interests. For many birth mothers and birth fathers, decisions too were made on their behalf within the prevailing social milieu.

Searching and perhaps ultimately reunion is a means for adopted persons to discover and exercise the control they never had because they had no say in the separation from their parents at birth. For birth parents, searching can help them rediscover the control they relinquished when the child was adopted. Thus, searching has a special significance for those wishing to address their loss and to find their whole selves.

For a birth father, searching means actively seeking (and obtaining) information about his adopted child, either through an adoption register, or via public records, which may culminate with the first contact, either by corresponding or in person. The phase beyond initial contact is usually known as reunion, although pedants will argue that because the birth father usually did not see the child prior to relinquishment, what in fact takes place is an initial meeting. I prefer to take the broader view that the father was present at conception and thus, taking a genetic perspective, contact does represent the door to reunion.

In some reunions between father and child, birth mothers have the opportunity to provide a facilitation role. If the birth father is not named on the birth certificate and their son or daughter asks the mother for the father's name, I maintain that the interests of the child should be paramount. Every adopted person has the right to know both of his or her birth parents. A child inherits genes, traits and medical history from their male and female antecedents. The birth mother and the birth father can each ensure that the adopted person knows the respective halves of their heritage. A birth mother's generosity may help the child to find the birth father, as well as an essential part of his or her identity.

It is apparent that much of the published data referred to below contain practical reasons for searching, which is sometimes the product of the closed questions posed in surveys. However, there is another factor, related to recognition that may contribute to the paucity of in-depth responses.

Andersen (1988) concluded that "the search is most fundamentally an expression of the wish to undo the trauma of separation" (p18). Rarely in the literature on the effects of adoption have I seen this fundamental acknowledged and explored. Some respondents approach this insight when they refer to the need to heal (for example Cicchini, 1993), but Andersen (1988 and 1989) is the only twentieth century researcher I know

The Invisible Men of Adoption

of who makes the ultimate connection. This suggests that many people questioned about the reasons for searching are perhaps either not aware of or prepared to grant deeper purposes. Whether or not those questioned have achieved reunion could be a factor that affects the insightfulness of an individual's answers. Whilst I bemoan the general lack of recognition that the searching undertaken by birth parents and adopted persons is primarily an attempt to resolve the grief resulting from loss, the secondary reasons well reported in the literature are nevertheless of interest, because they contribute to our understanding of the impact of separation on the family of origin. Grief resolution as the basis for personal and interpersonal integration is explored in more detail in the chapters that follow.

Searches by birth fathers

As expected, given the infrequent references to the experiences of birth fathers in the literature, there are few accounts of searches undertaken by birth fathers. The first overseas study dedicated to birth fathers was completed by Deykin, Patti and Ryan in 1988. They surveyed 125 American birth fathers, a self-selected sample drawn largely from adoption organisations and self-help groups. Given that the surveyed birth fathers had elected to come forward, suggesting they are the ones who have acknowledged the pain they suffered as a result of relinquishing a child to adoption, the conclusions reached by Deykin *et al* (1988) are perhaps not surprising. Almost all (96%) of the birth fathers had considered searching for their child; 67% had actually engaged in a search for the child, who in most cases, was now an adult. These were birth fathers who were aware of their losses. As in any study involving a self-selected sample, those who are not ready to reveal their feelings remain hidden. For this reason, Deykin *et al*'s 1988 findings cannot be applied to birth fathers in general. Nevertheless, this first major study of birth fathers' experiences highlighted that, like birth mothers, birth fathers could not forget

The Invisible Men of Adoption

their child. Relinquishment had been an important event in their lives. Deykin *et al* reached one controversial conclusion. They found that "search activity was highly associated with serious thoughts of taking the child back" (1988, p244). However, closer examination reveals that this conclusion resulted from analysis of the responses to the closed question, "Have you ever <u>seriously</u> thought of taking your child back?" This was the sole question in the survey that tackled the core emotional concern of responsibility towards the child. The need to discover a child's whereabouts and be assured about their well-being during all phases of their development may have "almost an obsessional quality" (Deykin *et al*, 1988, p244), but this does not necessarily correlate with an imperative to retrieve the child. The response to this specific question highlights the need to be cautious about interpreting the answers to surveys about searching. Because it can be a sensitive topic, some respondents may provide the 'expected' answer, particularly to a loaded question. (A negative answer could have been interpreted to mean that the participating birth fathers did not care about their adopted sons and daughters.)

Of Deykin *et al*'s 1988 finding that birth fathers harboured thoughts of physically reclaiming their child, Clapton says: "I found no evidence of this. A large majority of the men took pains to say that whilst they welcomed contact with their son or daughter, they also did not want to disrupt their child's life. It was made clear that whilst many of them saw themselves as the child's father, they did not see themselves as a 'dad' in respect of the child" (2001, p5). The men in Clapton's study did however report the following motives for seeking contact. A majority expressed a curiosity about how their child had 'turned out', half included a wish to expiate the guilt they now felt at having allowed the adoption to occur, several looked forward to the possibility of some sort of relationship with the now adult child (accepting that they could not replace the adoptive father) and a few acknowledged a need to fill in a part of themselves that was missing.

Cicchini (1993) also tested Deykin *et al*'s controversial finding in his study of West Australian birth fathers. Of thirty fathers surveyed, 77% had taken active steps to seek information about, or make contact with their child. The most heavily endorsed reasons for searching included:

Responsibility:
- "To ease my mind the child is OK" – 96%
- "Because I have a sense of responsibility for my child" – 91%
- "To explain the reasons and circumstances of relinquishment" – 74%

Curiosity/Need for Information:
- "To find out what my child looks like" – 91%
- "Curiosity on my part" – 74%

Reparation of Loss:
- "To have a relationship with my child" – 91%
- "To heal the hurt of being separated from my child" – 87%
- "To ease my sense of loss" – 83%

"To take child back" rated a lowly 13% (p19).

Cicchini (1993) further subdivides the factors that motivate a birth father's search into those that meet either the needs of the father or the child. The Need for Information and Reparation of Loss clearly relate to the father's needs, whilst Responsibility focuses on the child (although the first reason quoted above suggests also an opportunity for fathers to mitigate guilt). Cicchini notes that Curiosity has a special significance, because it represents "the deep importance that knowledge of one's ancestors, descendants and others with whom one has a biological link, has for human beings. It refers to a fundamental need to connect with, and know of, one's genetic relations" (p19). Birth father David Mendoza (Blau, 1993) expresses this need: "I thought my daughter might have some fantasies about what happened, and I wanted to let her know I'm here and she has some roots. I wanted her to know she has family, brothers and sisters, and maybe she might be curious to know who they are" (p78).

When Passmore and Coles asked the participants in their study of the adoption experiences of Australian and overseas birth fathers their primary reasons for searching, they found that "the most important motives seemed to be altruistic ones (*eg* motives that were concerned with the child's welfare) and motives that involved establishing a relationship with the child and providing the child with information (*eg* family background or the reasons for relinquishment). Motives concerning the birth father's own welfare (*eg* to help resolve loss and grief, to find peace, to relieve guilt) were also moderately important, but appeared further down the list" (2008, p6). One father gave his primary reason for searching as, "I came to find the grief debilitating", adding that in reaching out to his adult child, he expected to encounter another emotionally damaged person.

Silverman, Campbell, Patti and Style (1988) undertook a study of reunions between birth parents and adopted persons, from the birth parents' perspective. Subjects were contacted through adopted person and birth parent support organisations, an approach the authors readily acknowledge does not provide a representative sample. This is confirmed by the response to the questionnaires. Of the 246 birth parents who were contacted, only five were birth fathers. Silverman *et al* go on to say: "The results were examined, including and excluding the male respondents, and the presence or absence of fathers in the sample did not significantly affect the findings" (p523). Predictably, any unique birth father voice was swamped by the sheer volume of birth mother responses.

In a study undertaken by Howe and Feast (2000, p71), of 78 British adopted persons approached by birth relatives, 71% were first contacted by the birth mother and 23% by a birth sibling. Only 3% of contacts were initiated by birth fathers. There are data supplied by Witney (2003, p12) that the child (as adult) sought was twice as likely to be a daughter as a son. Whilst the reasons for this ratio are not explored in Witney's summary, it is possible that two factors may be influential, *viz* a father's protective instinct towards a daughter and a belief that a female may be more understanding about his part in the adoption.

Griffith (1991, Section 18, p2) highlights the difficulties New Zealand birth fathers have in initiating a search for their child. He writes: "Considering the numbers of birthparent applications, very few birthfathers are represented. This is not necessarily an indication of their interest, but merely that legally they are prevented from making application because their names are not entered in the birth registration." He goes on: "There is an indication from practice that **birthfathers are increasingly coming forward to make enquiries**, but are unable to apply under the Act because they cannot prove paternity" [emphasis in the reference]. This trend is backed by later figures. Griffith (personal communication, 2003) reports that the percentage of applications by birth fathers against the total of birth parent applications has risen from 5% in 1987 to figures that lie in the range of 15 to 21% between 1998 and 2002.

The seventeen men in Passmore and Coles' study who had searched for their adult children described a range of reunion experiences (Passmore and Coles, 2009). All of the birth fathers rated their first contact as satisfying, with several of the birth fathers feeling overjoyed or euphoric. Five birth fathers were also pleased that there was a mutual interest in contact. One birth father noted how glad he was that his son did not reject him, while another was happy that his daughter forgave him in the first letter that she wrote him. The interest or acceptance of other people (e.g., the adoptive parents or other family members) was also seen as a positive factor by three of the birth fathers. Three birth fathers had mixed emotions. While they were generally happy with the contact, these men also remembered feeling stressed, nervous, or sad. While the ongoing reunions were also rated as generally satisfying, a greater range of responses was noted. The two most common themes surrounding satisfaction in ongoing reunions were regular contact and shared experiences.

The Invisible Men of Adoption

Another satisfying aspect of the ongoing reunion was good communication. One participant found emailing particularly helpful in the first year of the reunion, as he found it easier to express himself using this mode of communication. Another noted that he and his child could speak openly on any subject. However, five birth fathers were dissatisfied with the amount of contact they had with their child. Three birth fathers noted the challenging nature of their reunions. While all three expressed some positives about the reunion, they also noted that it was "up and down, and hard work and expensive", "a difficult path", and like "walking on eggshells." One birth father also noted the lack of support from others, perceiving that his child's anger was being fuelled by other people.

Passmore and Coles observed that the birth fathers in their study had usually known of the child's existence since the pregnancy, and in many cases, had thought about the child since the relinquishment. The men had sometimes spent many years searching for their child before they were finally able to meet. Thus, compared with their adult children (only six of the twenty reunited adopted persons in this study had actively searched for their birth father), it is likely that the birth fathers had been contemplating a reunion for longer and may have been better prepared for contact (Passmore and Coles, 2009).

Rob Brown writes of his search in an article published in 2002. He speaks of fear, guilt and confusion preventing him from taking any action for seventeen years. When he did initiate a search, he was deterred by the barriers that he encountered. He also realised that he liked the idea of finding his son, but was frightened by the prospect of being rejected. In 2000, at the time his first born son was 27, Rob used his 'accident' to illustrate a talk about contraception to the eldest teenaged son of his marriage. A year later, this son expressed an interest in finding out about his older half-sibling. Rob reactivated the search and found the name and overseas address of his oldest son. Still apprehensive about making the first contact, he asked a professional mediator to act on his behalf. Rob's reaction to being told that his son welcomed contact from him was "I ... cried ... with joy, sadness, excitement ... I jumped around the house and sang" (Brown, 2002, p8). When Rob telephoned his son that evening, he experienced an overwhelming relief. "He actually wanted to know me" (*ibid*).

I know of but one non-fiction book-length account (*Ithaka*) of a birth father's search, albeit written in the third person. It is provided by Sarah Saffian, an adopted person who was searched for by her birth parents. As the birth parents married several years after Sarah was adopted, their search was a joint one. However, during the search Adam and Hannah corresponded separately with their daughter. After an initial phone call made by him, the reader 'hears' Adam's viewpoint from his letters, which cover three years. Early in their correspondence, he apologises for having caught his daughter unprepared, but sees a benefit for her: "I'm glad you were spared some of the anxiety of wondering what you would find" [if Sarah had initiated the search] (Saffian, 1998, p21). In subsequent letters, he is transparent about his relationship with Hannah before and after Sarah's adoption. Adam shows concern for his daughter: "We worried and wondered and hoped for the best for you, but never considered intruding on your upbringing" (p157) and "The major factor in our searching for and in our communications with you has always been how you felt, your well-being" (p172). Responding to Sarah's concerns that he is pushing for reunion, he draws on his upbringing by guardians: "... because I am so sure, due to my own experiences, that it is good to deal as soon as possible with emotional pain and good to learn about your origins, I display greater urgency. I'm aware of the mistakes I made in my own life by delaying these things, and I don't want you to do the same. That's where I'm coming from" (p173). Later in their correspondence Adam reflects: "Sarah, finding you, talking to you, seeing your pictures, writing to you and reading your letters has been astonishing" (p219). Always present is his concern that they may never meet: "It would be wonderful to see you, but it would be terrible to take away your control of the reunion and to

The Invisible Men of Adoption

have you feel that your space is being invaded" (p233). When Sarah does decide she is ready to meet her birth parents, the reportage is hers and Adam is treated in the narrative as a bystander. Sarah's focus is clearly on Hannah and the full sisters and brother she is meeting for the first time.

Searches for birth fathers

There is a common theme that pervades the accounts of adopted persons searching for their birth fathers. Birth fathers typically are the subject of an adopted person's search <u>after</u> the birth mother has been located and contacted.

The Adoption and Family Records Service (AFRS) in Victoria, in their publication *Adoption: Myth and Reality* (Victorian Government Department of Human Services, 2009) points out there is a practical reason for this sequence. Because birth fathers, historically were not named on the birth certificate, many adopted people are dependent on the birth mother for information about the identity of their birth father. "This may be difficult to obtain if the birth mother still believes there are strong reasons for her non-disclosure of the birth father's name" (p12). Again, we see evidence of the impact of the quality of the relationship between the birth parents having an influence upon the involvement of the birth father, post-adoption. It is the view of AFRS that even though birth fathers may not always know that a child was conceived and born as a result of their relationship with the birth mother, "experience indicates that they generally respond positively to an approach from the adopted person" (p13). VANISH (1998) explores these reasons further. Noting that, "for the natural mother, there may be unresolved issues involving the natural father", "the natural mother may feel that:
1. He deserted her and that he has no right to know this child,
2. The circumstances around conception have been difficult,
3. She has a strong desire to protect her child from the hurt she herself had experienced from him,

The Invisible Men of Adoption

4. He may not know she became pregnant if the relationship had broken down before she was aware she was pregnant" (p105).

Any negative feelings may be projected by the birth mother on to the enquiring adopted person. She may convey, whether directly or by implication, that 'he didn't want to know you then, so why should he now?' This is the hurt response of a birth mother that reflects but one aspect of the 'unfinished business' depicted on the Adoption Sandwich diagram. For birth mothers, 'unfinished business' may range from a desire to have it out with the birth father (to proclaim her rage and her pain), to a suppressed longing to explore 'what could have been'.

Gediman and Brown (1991) pick up on this theme of birth mother responses, noting that,

> "when adoptees want to search for their birthfather, the best information where to begin usually resides with the birthmother, but asking for her assistance can be a touchy matter, especially if she fails to volunteer it. The feelings she has about the birthfather, good or bad, are destined to be strong, and probably include a mixture of hurt and anger that remains unresolved. He could have been her high school sweetheart – a boy she had been seeing for months or years – or he could have been a more casual affair, even a 'one night stand'. He could have been her first sexual partner, even her first sexual experience. He could have been someone she loved and wanted to marry, or someone she never would have considered for marriage. It's possible he was even her husband, maybe soon to be (or just recently) estranged. And beyond what he meant to her in any of these ways, his attitude and behaviour during her pregnancy, good or bad, is not something she is likely to forget" (pp170–171).

Tugendhat (1992) is another who notes the criticality of the relationship between the birth parents, but not from the conventional point of view of the willingness or otherwise of the birth mother to release identifying information about the birth father. She writes: "Even if a man has not told his present wife or family about the child he fathered many years earlier, he is not necessarily going to reject that child if he is contacted ... A father's attitude is likely to depend on his former feelings for the mother. If he felt good about her, his response is likely to be positive. But if he had been ignored, or bullied by her family, his response may be negative" (p26). Here the relationship between the birth parents is seen from the point of view of the birth father, conditioned by the attitude of the birth mother and/or her family towards him. This is the birth father as an acted upon figure.

Betty Jean Lifton (1994) iterates a similar message: "The birth father's response to the adoptee will, as with the mother, depend on many factors: his relationship with the mother at the time of conception; his loyalty to her during pregnancy and delivery; his involvement in the adoption decision; whether or not he has kept the child a secret over the years; and whether he feels he is in a secure place in his present relationships" (p192). Lifton (1994) also reinforces the common view that adopted persons block out thoughts of searching for the birth father "until after they find the birth mother" (p191). She goes on: "If the reunion with the mother proves satisfying, the adoptee may have less emotional investment in the father" (*ibid*) and "If the adoptee has been unacknowledged by the birth mother, or is disappointed in her, there is always the second chance with the birth father" (p192). Note again, the birth father is the secondary not primary figure and sometimes the second resort.

There are factors specific to birth mothers' experiences that may cause them distress when asked by their adopted child to talk about the birth father. The quality of the relationship between the parents before, during and after the conception of the child may have been ambivalent or threatening. In some cases, the birth mother may have been under the age of consent, meaning that the father was liable for prosecution, or the pregnancy may have resulted from rape or incest. Consequently, a birth mother may be reluctant to disclose the nature of the original relationship between the birth parents. If the birth mother has scant information about the birth father, or cannot recall past events, she may feel ashamed and therefore avoid talking about him. In many instances, the birth parents enjoyed a loving relationship, but because of the intervention of others, often the parents of the birth mother, they were kept apart during the pregnancy, the birth and the adoption. In this situation, subsequent enquiries made by the adult child may reactivate the spectre of 'unfinished business' for one or both birth parents. The birth mother may prefer not to revisit the pain of her separation from the birth father. If the birth mother feels insecure in the relationship she has achieved through reunion with her child, she may be reluctant to share knowledge about the identity of the father, for fear of 'losing her child again'. In this circumstance, the birth father may be perceived as a fresh threat, in that the child might establish a closer relationship with him than with the birth mother.

What is typically the primary (and sometimes the only) reunion presents interpersonal challenges for birth mothers and adopted persons. It takes courage and compassion on the part of both people to take the next step and include the birth father.

There are some mothers who at the first asking, may feel disinclined to discuss the father. However, after addressing suppressed memories and paying attention to her wounded feelings, a birth mother may feel better disposed to provide information about the birth father. The tolerance and patience of adopted persons may give birth mothers the space to process their pain, thus potentially clearing the path to the birth father.

One adopted person whose search for her birth father is documented, is Australian writer and art lecturer Susanna de Vries (Bradley, 2001), who, on the death of her adoptive father, discovered documents identifying the man who had fathered her in 1935. She located "a regular Don Juan ... who women fell for enthusiastically ... I can't say he was terribly interested in me; he kept talking about his own career." In a reversal of the normal sequence, de Vries subsequently searched for her mother, but when she attempted to make contact, she discovered that her mother's funeral had taken place two weeks previously.

The Invisible Men of Adoption

Another account is of Peter, aged 45 at the time of his interview, recorded in a chapter called *Boys who miss out*, in a section headed *Absent Fathers* in the book *On Their Own*, by Rex McCann (2000). After noting that: "The feeling for the birth father is often a vague loss, hard to make peace with" and "... the desire to know where one comes from is deep, and for men, their biological father is an important key – even if they have never met him", McCann goes on to record Peter's story:

> "... But I can't recall early memories of my adopted father. Maybe this gave me a longing to know more about my real father.
> What was he like? What did he do? Would he know me? Did I look like him? These were all questions nobody would answer, questions that would usually elicit a growling or a smacking if they persisted.
> I always felt alone in that family. Most times I had unlimited freedom and from an early age spent many evenings and weekends alone in the bush camping and giving my father-fantasies full rein. I was always wondering what he was like, and trying to be a man like him.
> ... when I was sixteen [I] joined the armed forces ... I still felt a hollowness about not knowing who my real father was. I would often cry in private with the frustration of not knowing. When I left the forces I married and had children and that feeling of longing dissipated somewhat as I coped with married life. But when we divorced I longed for knowledge of my real father again and I turned to professional agencies to trace him.
> One agency called to let me know they had traced the family he now had and were going to discreetly find out more personal details before arranging any meetings. Two days after the first call they rang and informed me I had three half-brothers and four half-sisters, but my real father had died some eight years previously from a heart attack.
> It's now a couple of years on and I still think of him, not so much with sadness now, but more with understanding and a

The Invisible Men of Adoption

sense of identity, which is being reinforced by the step-family who are now talking to me about him" (pp20–21).

Although in Schaefer (1991) it is the birth father who makes the initial verbal contact, Jack, the son is the one who, at short notice, having already booked the flights, arranges their first meeting. Jack describes a chain of reactions ranging from calmness before the aircraft landed, through feeling "so weak he didn't think he could get out of the seat" to being "very comfortable" with the reunion (p275). Having met first his birth mother, then his birth father, Jack reports that he "felt free to love his [adoptive] parents even more", a common reaction, according to Schaefer (1991, p276).

For a few, birth mother and birth father are discovered concurrently. When Jenny Watkins (Watkins and Reynolds, 2000) wrote to the son she had lost through adoption thirty years previously and Robert responded, he was contacting both his birth parents, for Jenny had married Robert's birth father.

Gediman and Brown (1991) explore the mixed blessings for an adopted person of discovering that the birth parents are husband and wife.

> "On the positive side, there's the exhilaration of finding both parents at once and the joyful knowledge that they must have loved one another. You're a 'love child', as one daughter happily put it. Also, any siblings you meet are likely to be full-siblings, not half, making the genetic tie between these brothers and sisters complete. Then too, you don't have to worry about whether your birthmother is harbouring hateful feelings toward a man who left her in the lurch, or whether her current husband will be threatened if she helps you search. On the negative side though, you may feel especially betrayed to discover that their lives rejoined after the adoption and went forward without you" (p174).

In an earlier book, Lifton (1988) referred to the search sequence in these terms: "Tracking down [the] father is the last

The Invisible Men of Adoption

stage of the Search, but one does not embark on it until one has absorbed the reunion with the mother" (p152). She puts the hierarchy into perspective when she says: "I call the quest for the father the Mini-Search" (p153). Clapton confirms this hierarchy, stating: "It is my personal experience that whilst it is the case that the search for a birth mother came first, interest in and a search for the birth father grew in the following months and years that followed this first contact with a birth parent" (2001, p5).

Down the Track, a collection of personal stories recording the outcomes of adoption reunions is notable for the number of adopted persons who, having met their birth mother, state that "the only gap that remains in my life is that I haven't met my natural father" (NSW Committee on Adoption, Inc, 1990, p61). The reasons articulated for not having achieved reunion with the birth father vary, but include deferring to the real or perceived feelings of the birth mother and an unwillingness of the birth mother to reveal his identity.

Sachdev (1992), referred to in Howe and Feast (2000, p18), reported that only a few of those adopted persons participating in his study expressed any desire to meet their birth father. Only 20% said they had ever thought about their birth father.

On the subject of adopted persons and birth fathers knowing each other, the VANISH Resource Book (VANISH, 1998) is quite unequivocal. It advocates contact between adopted persons and their birth fathers. "**We believe that adopted people have a right to know their father**. We encourage women to consider that if the adoptee needs to 'know' about her, then he/she also needs to have the same knowledge of the natural father. Adoptees can make their own decisions about that information" (p106) [emphasis in the reference].

Contemporary statistics from post-adoption service providers in Australia and New Zealand indicate that more men (particularly adopted persons) are initiating searches than previously. There is a trend towards parity in the numbers of male and female searchers. The increased involvement of male adopted persons is most welcome, particularly for those birth fathers (and birth mothers) whose child is a son.

Those who do not wish to have contact

There are those, both birth parents and adopted persons, who have no intention of initiating a search and/or do not wish to be contacted. They deserve to be considered, although by maintaining their avowed intention to remain outside the search/reunion process, they and, in particular birth parents, are a difficult grouping to analyse. Nevertheless, their viewpoints are recorded in the literature.

The Victorian Government Department of Human Services (2009) has documented some of the reasons why a minority of birth mothers decide not to have contact with their child, when they are approached. These are:

– "Fear of rejection or blame by the adopted person.

– Disclosure of their child's existence would threaten the stability of their present family, particularly if the family had not been told of the adoption.

– Overwhelming feelings of guilt at the prospect of meeting their child.

– Feeling unable to cope with meeting their child, after the grief and pain of the pregnancy and adoption." (pp11–12).

Griffith (1991) recorded similar reasons for birth mothers not initiating a search, with the addition of: "Feelings of unworthiness relating to the stigma of having given birth ex-nuptially and guilt from having given the child for adoption" and the moral obligation to adhere to the commitment made at the time of the adoption that they would never attempt to find their child – "They feel the change in the law does not release them from this oath given on the Bible" (Section 18, p1). Reasonably, most of these defences could be expected to apply to birth fathers as well.

The Invisible Men of Adoption

Referring to adopted persons, the Victorian Government Department of Human Services has this to say:

> "Some adopted people never feel the need to seek information or make contact, or do so later in their lives following a particular crisis or event. Fear of hurting the adoptive parents is extensively documented. The decision to seek information may create feelings of disloyalty towards the adoptive parents. Many people face the dilemma of searching now and perhaps hurting the adoptive parents, or waiting until later – when it may be too late.
> Adopted people often fear their birth parents' reactions and are worried about hurting them. Fear of rejection is almost always present. Some people are also afraid of what they may discover about their birth families" (2009, p9).

They could have been conceived as a result of rape. The princess of their fantasy may turn out to be a prostitute, or destitute, or in a mental institution.

In their study of adopted persons, Howe and Feast (2000) comment on the paucity of data about those who do not search. "Although a growing amount is known about those who do search, much less is known about those who do not seek further information about their adoption or who do not actively desire contact with a birth relative" (p57). To redress this balance, Howe and Feast undertook to contact adult adopted persons who had been approached by birth relatives. Howe and Feast categorise this group (78 in all) as non-searchers. This term is somewhat of a misnomer, because it can be construed to mean that they have chosen not to search, when in fact they are the recipients of requests for contact. They are passive searchees rather than definite non-searchers. This distinction becomes apparent in the data presented. Forty-two per cent said they had thought about searching before their birth relative (predominantly birth mother) made contact. Half of this subset, sixteen adopted persons, had taken preliminary steps to try to locate their birth relative before being contacted themselves.

The Invisible Men of Adoption

Howe and Feast (2000) questioned all 78 adopted persons in this grouping about their reasons for not activating a search. The dominant responses were:
– feel that my adoptive parents are my real parents (47%),
– did not want to upset adoptive parents (44%), and
– scared information might be upsetting/unpleasant (31%) (p59).
For eight (10%) of the adult non-searchers who chose not to have direct contact with their birth relative, initial attempts to subject them to outreach were not viewed well. For some, the request for contact was experienced as intrusive and unwelcome, as causing anger and upsetting the adoptive parents. Yet, six out of the eight said it felt good to know the birth relative had not forgotten them. All eight viewed themselves as secure, complete persons with a positive view of themselves.

There are similarities here with three non-searching adopted persons, who are the subject of a paper by Roche (1999). Her study participants had made a conscious decision not to search for their birth parents. Roche (p13) concluded, contrary to an expectation, that as non-searchers, they were "more likely to uphold a moral position of maintaining loyalty to their adoptive parents" (against searchers having "a strong tendency towards self-discovery"), her three subjects held both positions simultaneously. However, the 'self-discovery' described relates to immersion in external activities, through the roles respectively of painter, counsellor and nurturer. From the material provided in Roche's paper, there is no sense of an inner journey. No evidence is provided that this small sample of non-searcher adopted persons are living fulfilling lives because they have chosen not to have contact with their birth parents. More pertinent are the findings in Roche's paper that support previous studies. All participants said they would react positively to contact if it came from the birth parent. Loyalty to the adoptive parents was a reason expressed by the threesome, all over the age of forty, for not searching. A determination to protect parents who are now aged is evident here. The reactions of these non-searchers bear out Seitz's (2000) observation "that even when an adoptee claims to be a non-searcher, they are at some level, conscious or not, curious about their origins" (p100).

Less ambivalent is this letter from an adopted person, obviously a passionate non-searcher (Sorosky *et al* 1989):

> "I, for one, would highly resent the intrusion by my biological parents into my present life, for they mean absolutely nothing to me. I feel about them the same way I do about the stranger on the street – general indifference. Quite frankly, I really do not understand why there is such a problem. What difference does it make whose seed started what entity? ... I feel pity for adoptees who spend so much of their life dwelling on the identity of their biological parents rather than living. To have an individual believe that such knowledge is essential to their self-identity is tragic" (p137).

Adopted person Betty Jean Lifton (1988) has this to say about the avid non-searcher:

> "It seems that militant nonsearchers (*sic*) have absorbed society's negative image of what they might find if they searched. One hears them say 'I don't want to rock the boat' or 'Why should I open a can of worms?' They accept the position that it is an act of disloyalty to the adoptive parents. It becomes a moral issue in which they see the searcher as an ingrate, just as the searcher sees them as an Uncle Tom. 'Our adoptive parents accepted us for what we were with no questions asked', they might say, or 'Meeting my natural mother would be an unnecessary trauma in my life as well as hers. I don't think there could be a more selfish quest than this' " (p75).

Lifton then makes her judgment:

> "Nonsearchers, for all their sense of righteousness and loyalty, have always seemed to me self-denigrating. There is the implication that they don't have a right to rock their own boat, to open their own can of worms. They seem to accept

> they don't have a right to own their own heritage. We see such internalised guilt in them that even if their adoptive parents should sanction a search, it would be hard for them to follow through. It is as if they have a will not to know" (*ibid*).

These are the adopted persons who assert that they are content with their lives and see no need to seek a reunion with birth parents. By taking this stance, they are equating the birth parents with discontent and disruption, a simplistic position most birth mothers and birth fathers would find horrifying and unwarranted.

Neil Fredman, an adopted person writing in *The Age* of 19 November 2001, illustrates these attitudes. He concedes that thoughts for his birth mother are only fleeting, which is in accord with his assertion that adoptive parents "provide a life" for adopted persons and "are the unsung heroes of the adoption process." Fredman (2001) states that he has "no desire to search for my birth mother." He equates searching with upheaval, claiming that "you should never interfere with your life to that extent due to curiosity." Fredman exhibits a profound unwillingness to admit that adoption has affected his life. Further, he displays a lack of understanding about the issues that face parents who have lost a child through adoption, culminating, for many, in a need to search. He sees a reunion between birth parent and child as risky for the adoptive parents because they face the possibility of losing their child. Ultimately, Fredman claims that it is better that adopted persons do not acknowledge that adoption has had an impact on their lives. As stated by him, "... this [admission] stops us from the self-analysis needed to become better people." Research and anecdotal accounts demonstrate that many, many adopted persons, adoptive parents and birth parents hold the opposing view. It is through self-analysis that they have come to understand how adoption has affected their lives and, as a result, become more rounded persons, the better for having the courage to admit to and confront their feelings.

The Invisible Men of Adoption

Less strident than the militant non-searchers are those adopted persons who use the excuse 'I don't blame my birth parents for my situation' to avoid searching. This is a selfish response, because, by hiding behind these sentiments, adopted persons have made the choice not to inform their birth parents that they absolve them of any perceived wrongdoing. Without this reassurance, birth parents are likely to continue to carry negative feelings about the loss of their child. Birth parents would prefer to know, for their own peace of mind, that their offspring does not blame them for being adopted.

Another reason for not searching, referred to in Howe and Feast (2000) and used by 23% of their sample of non-searchers, is "... there was no point as [my] birth parents had already rejected me by placing me for adoption" (p59) makes the dangerous, often false assumption that birth parents were in total control of the decisions that led to the loss of their child. Birth parents deserve to be given the opportunity to respond to this accusation. Without this dialogue, the myth of voluntary relinquishment is bound to be perpetuated, to the detriment of the well-being of the adopted person and the birth parents.

Brodzinsky *et al* (1993, p102) identify four ways to resolve the 'identity crisis', which conventionally begins in adolescence and may continue beyond. For adolescent adopted persons, this period is complicated by their having one family they know (the adoptive family) and one that is a mystery to them. The identity issues fall into four, non-sequential categories:

1. Identity achievement: The individual explores various values and ideologies, then makes a commitment to a particular identity. Among adopted persons, identity achievers tend to be those whose adoptive families have allowed open discussion about adoption.
2. Moratorium: Essentially, this is a state of flux, of non-resolution and discomfort, which is a stepping stone to the other states. Adopted persons whose parents have not been open with them or who do not have access to information about themselves fall into this category.

3. Identity foreclosure: The individual appears to have achieved an identity, but it is one taken on prematurely and to please others. Adopted persons in this pattern often deny what adoption means to them and claim to have no curiosity. (Sorosky *et al*'s passionate non-searcher, quoted above, is likely to be in identity foreclosure.) On further questioning, they often turn out to have taken on their adoptive parents' attitudes towards adoption, rather than making their own choices.

4. Identity diffusion: The identity diffuse individual flounders without a strong foundation based on morals, career, or role models, to be able to discover where they are going, who they are. Adopted persons in identity diffusion are in a state of limbo, not interested in either adoptive or birth families and unable to develop a plan to advance. They are rudderless.

Adopted person non-searchers fall into the last three categories. Moratorium and identity diffusion are states of ambivalence and uncertainty; identity foreclosure is a stand against acknowledging the impact of adoption on the individual and protecting the feelings of adoptive parents. It is important to note, that whilst this development of identity can be applied to adolescence in general, for adopted persons there is the extra layering of the two selves, one inherited from the family of origin and one acquired.

For those birth parents who are waiting to be found, all is not lost. As Lifton (1988) acknowledges, "the fact that adoptees ... are not searching now does not mean that they will not be searching in the future" (p77). The change is likely to require going inside oneself and making a conscious choice. For those in moratorium, identity foreclosure, or identity diffusion, this may be a difficult, although by no means impossible transition.

Several researchers have written about the importance of intense experiences in adoptees' lives as catalysts for searching. Transitions from adolescence to adulthood, from being single to becoming married, from marriage to divorce, the death of a partner, as well as the milestones of parenthood and the death of one or both the adoptive parents are significant events. The need for genetic information may become critical, sometimes at the behest of the partner, when an adopted person decides to marry or to start a family. For an adopted woman, pregnancy and childbirth may create an acute identification with the physical and psychological pain that her birth mother experienced during labour and relinquishment. The death of an adoptive parent may free the adoptee from the feeling, that, by searching, they are betraying those who raised them. One of these life-changing episodes may provide the external catalyst for adopted persons to begin the internal work.

CHAPTER 10

Personal effects

"There is only one journey. Going inside yourself." — Rainer Maria Rilke

I am convinced that facing and accepting the truth about parent–child separation and adoption is empowering and that the alternative of denial is debilitating. For birth parents, accepting that the loss of a child through adoption has influenced the way they have lived their lives since that decision was taken is a significant realisation. For adopted persons, acknowledging their origins is accepting their innate curiosity. Understanding their background is a key to integrating and validating their two selves, the birth and the adopted.

Adopted person the Reverend Thomas Brosnan, in his keynote address to the 1996 National Maternity and Adoption Conference in San Antonio, Texas, reinforced the link between curiosity and wholeness when he said: "Belonging and identity are synonymous for the adoptee, but he must initiate his search, or at least acknowledge the desire to search for his identity, *in order for the healing to begin."* He was given a standing ovation [Note: emphasis in the original, from *issues* Number 3, 1997, p11].

For male adopted persons, there may be another factor that comes into play. Just as a birth father experiences a social expectation that he demonstrate responsibility by protecting the mother and her unborn child, so a male adopted person may feel a compulsion to display the essence of his maleness by shielding his adoptive mother, from, for example, a perceived intrusion by birth parents. Whilst this is not a healthy response, because it suggests

The Invisible Men of Adoption

an adoptive family in which the birth parents are held in scant regard, which in turn blocks the prospect of a mutually beneficial reunion between a son and his birth parents, it is perhaps not unexpected, when seen from the viewpoint of a sense of responsibility toward the female who has provided the nurturing during his upbringing. The adoptive mother has an important role to play here, one of assuring her son that she accepts that he is a member of families with which he has and does not have blood links; that his adoptive family does not lay exclusive claim to him.

Protectiveness may also influence how a male adopted person perceives his birth parents. If he believes that the birth father abandoned the birth mother and thus forced her, as the victim, to relinquish her child, *ie* him, his anger may be directed at the birth father. He may regard the birth mother in a more sympathetic light.

Birth fathers have been called double abandoners. Some fathers, including me, internalised this epithet, because it encapsulated the way they felt about themselves, as a consequence of their actions. However, this does not mean that birth fathers have ever rejected the birth mother or their child. Birth fathers would be shocked to hear that their not being there could be construed to mean a permanent renouncement of the mother and their child. It is helpful for others to recognise that, in common with many birth mothers, birth fathers acted under duress, making decisions that precluded an awareness of the long term ramifications of being 'separated from family'.

Considerations about the impact of adoption necessarily embrace the nexus between abandonment and love. This apparently confusing conjunction can appear threatening to all parties. How a birth mother can give up her child is a dilemma that may consume both people. Some adopted persons fear intimacy, because getting close to another raises the spectre of a second perceived rejection. When an adopted person searches for their birth parents, adoptive parents may feel that the love they have provided is not enough and that they risk being forsaken for a mother and a father who offer consanguinity and identity settlement.

At a rational level, it does not make sense that we would hurt those whom we care about. Abandonment, however, is an emotional word that carries negative connotations, the most potent of which may be the belief that it is permanent and irredeemable. Abandonment can embrace damaging perceptions and misconceptions, frequently at the expense of what lies quietly hidden.

I believe that searching for the person(s) separated from you by adoption, accompanied by the search for self is a positive sign that you have, from a position of self-awareness, elected to own your decisions and actions; you have made a conscious choice to minimise the influence of constraining external factors. It represents a transformation from selfishness to unselfishness, reinforced by a recognition that you are willing to consider allowing the person(s) separated from you by adoption back into your life, so that you are in a position to participate in their healing and they in yours. People who refuse to meet the other are not in a position to offer healing or to be healed.

The parting of birth parent and child at or soon after birth, results in grief. Those separated by adoption may experience the burden of guilt and the fear of rejection. They may query their personal identity and have reservations about their capacity to maintain a relationship, because getting close may re-enact the primary loss. If the birth parents and their son or daughter are prepared to meet and to share their feelings about these fundamental matters, bringing their own perspective and a willingness to listen to the other, then the prospects of an enduring reunion are enhanced. The original separation and consequent loss produced these issues; now they are providing the catalyst to bring parent and child together again.

From birth parents and adult children separated by adoption, the reports about the impact on themselves of the search and reunion phase of their personal journeys are overwhelmingly positive. As extolled by two adopted persons: "Adult children

The Invisible Men of Adoption

who search have chosen to give up the denial" (Small, 1987, p40) and "I am more self-aware – I feel that I know myself better and more positively now that my genetic gaps have been filled in" (Stephen Ferguson in Robinson, 2000a, p207); in other words – from committed beginnings, great benefits ensue.

The Invisible Men of Adoption

The Invisible Men of Adoption

Trio

CHAPTER 11

Introducing a fresh perspective

"Life can only be understood backwards; but it must be lived forwards." –
Soren Aaby Kierkegaard

In the third quarter of the twentieth century, when the numbers of adoptions peaked, the belief that an adoption benefited the participants and provided a convenient solution for all was accompanied by an expectation that the birth parents, the adopted person and the adoptive parents would continue with their lives as if the separation and placement had never occurred. Rarely, if ever, were the consequences of the splitting of a family of origin discussed before an adoption took place, if indeed they were acknowledged. Advice from parents, social and church workers may have been, on occasions, well meaning, but rarely were their words informed by practical experience. This lack of comprehension did not prevent social workers and others from assuring birth parents that giving up a child was in the mother's, the father's and the child's best interests, at the time and forever.

In particular, there was a presumption that mothers, who had experienced the ignominy of giving birth to a child out of wedlock and been relieved of the evidence, would also be released from an emotional attachment to the child. Some members of the public believed that it was obvious that the mother could not care for her child, otherwise she would have resisted all the advice and kept the baby. In a social setting where illegitimacy was kept a dark secret, mothers (and fathers) who lost their children through adoption were discouraged from ever revealing how they felt about their loss. As a result of these falsehoods and society's condemnation of their 'mistake', many birth parents believed that they were failures when they found that they could not forget their child.

It took investigations by authors such as Winkler and van Keppel (1984) and Robinson (2003) to overturn these unkind fables, as they applied to birth mothers. These studies revealed that mourning the loss of a child to adoption was to be expected and encouraged, if healing was to occur. Coles (2004) discussed the impact of adoption on birth fathers, identifying the unique qualities of this experience. Likewise, studies by Lifton (1988), Brodzinsky *et al* (1993) and Verrier (1993) revealed the legacy of the original parent–child separation on adopted persons, in particular the breaking of the primal mother–child bond. The overwhelming conclusion of all of this research is that the splitting of the family of origin does not provide the lasting pain-free solution, contrary to the assumptions of many people without an adoption experience of their own.

Instead, there have been and continue to be significant issues of well-being for many of those separated by an adoption. Kaplan and Silverstein (1991) highlighted what they called the Seven Core Issues of Adoption, *viz* Loss, Rejection, Guilt/Shame, Grief, Identity, Intimacy and Control, as they apply to members of the traditional Adoption Triangle, in which birth mothers represent birth parents. For the sake of alignment, I applied the same model, in which each attribute has an equal weighting, to birth fathers (see Chapter 4: Finding the father within).

In taking this approach, the seven core issues were considered and described individually. Hitherto, they have not been reviewed for possible linkages and sequencing. In what follows in this section, I have opted for a cause and effect approach, one not explored previously. I believe that this fresh perspective on the consequences of adoption is aligned with what members of the family of origin actually experience.

CHAPTER 12

The long and wounding road

"Adoption is a lifelong process, but it does not have to be a lifetime sentence."
— Gediman and Brown (1991, p254)

In *Ever After: Fathers and the Impact of Adoption,* I concluded that fundamentally my search was both for my son and my self; by undertaking this quest I attempted to resolve the grief caused by the initial separation. Robinson (2004), in *Adoption and Recovery: Solving the mystery of reunion*, addresses this dichotomy in a different way. She explores the two aspects of the parent and the child working to mend the damage (grief) caused by the severance, which she calls 'personal recovery' and 'interpersonal recovery'. As the terms suggest, the former relates to the self and the latter applies to reunion with the adult adopted child. Medical definitions centre on grief as the normal *ie* anticipated reaction to a loss. There are references to losses being physical, social or occupational and common emotional reactions, which may include denial, anger, guilt and anxiety. Thus, there is a demonstrable link between loss and grief, with the former the trigger for the latter. These foundations provide the ideal framework within which to re-evaluate the most frequently recorded emotional aspects of an adoption, to move beyond Kaplan and Silverstein's treatment of the key issues of Loss, Rejection, Guilt/Shame, Grief, Identity, Intimacy and Control as discrete entities.

Firstly, the Grief referred to by Kaplan and Silverstein has a narrower, sorrow based focus. Furthermore, who we are and what we think of ourselves (*ie* Identity) are surely related to the impact of the other matters (Rejection, Guilt/Shame, Intimacy and Control) upon us. These linkages suggest start and end points (Loss and Identity) of a fresh approach to evaluating the legacy of an adoption, made under the umbrella of the broadened definition of Grief as diverse responses to the initial Loss.

I contend that the key issues are best considered as a continuum that begins with the separation, which causes reactions (or wounds) that must be (ad)dressed before recovery is possible. I have depicted this in Figure 3 (Parent and Child – Separation and Integration), which displays the repercussions of an adoption. For the sake of simplicity, I have shown the birth parents as an entity, overall, the emphasis is on the separation of parent and child. However, where appropriate in the text, the unique experiences of each birth parent are identified.

The initial parting results in a loss for the birth parents and their child. For each person, the primary loss may produce a range of grief reactions embracing denial, anger, guilt, shame and diverse fears, which require a resolve (commitment) to take action before recovery is possible. The manifestations of grief are led by denial, because, if this response is rigid, it is unlikely that the individual will be in a position to acknowledge the other facets. Not every person who has suffered an adoption loss necessarily experiences all of the aspects of grief, nor need they acknowledge and address them in a designated order. For example, a birth mother may have always recognised her loss and the accompanying sorrow, *ie* for her, denial is irrelevant. Instead, residual guilt may be her paramount concern. Later, perhaps, she may deal with her anger issues, related to the lack of support she experienced before and after the adoption took place.

To mend, the birth parent and the (adult) child undertake a programme of reconciliation and repair. The search is both for their 'whole' selves and the other person. This journey, incorporating the decision to change from being acted upon to taking action, is displayed below.

The Invisible Men of Adoption

Figure 3: **Parents and Child — Separation and Integration**

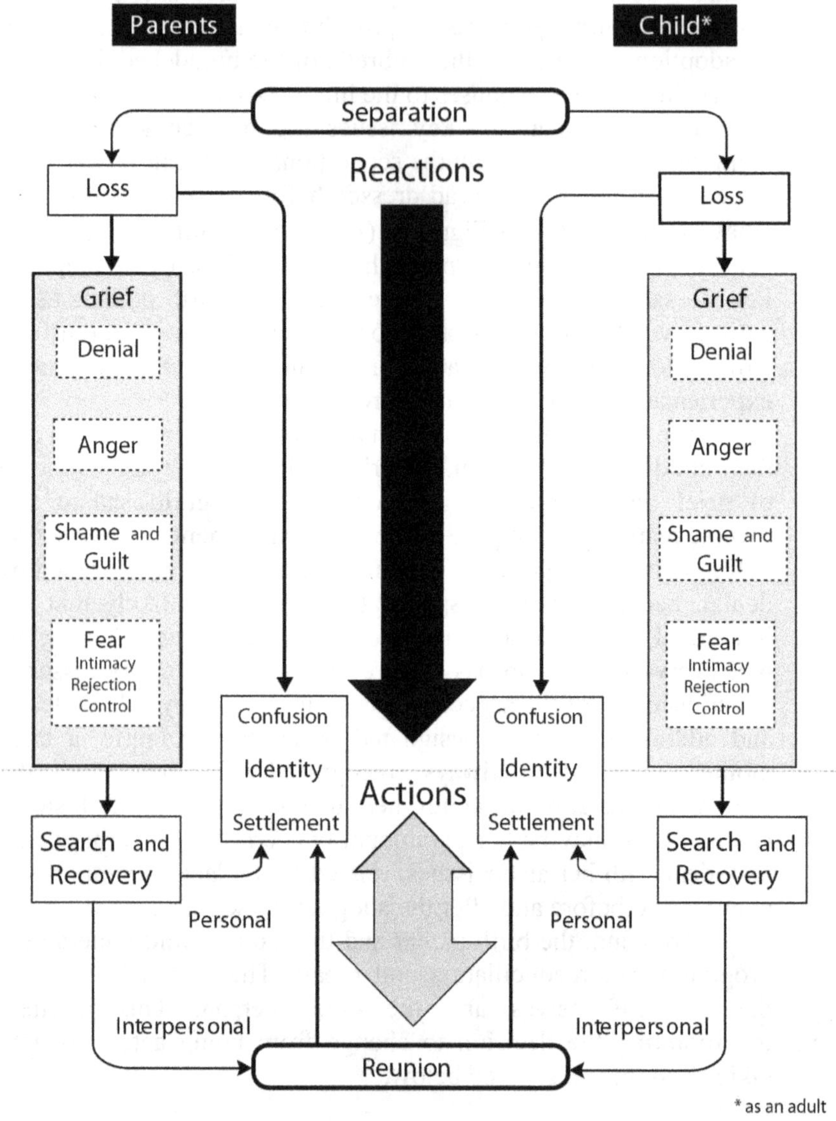

Parents | **Child***

Separation

Reactions

Parents side:
- Loss
  - Grief
    - Denial
    - Anger
    - Shame and Guilt
    - Fear — Intimacy, Rejection, Control
- Search and Recovery
- Confusion / Identity / Settlement

Child side:
- Loss
  - Grief
    - Denial
    - Anger
    - Shame and Guilt
    - Fear — Intimacy, Rejection, Control
- Search and Recovery
- Confusion / Identity / Settlement

Actions

Personal → Confusion / Identity / Settlement

Interpersonal → Reunion

* as an adult

The Invisible Men of Adoption

Some people affected by adoption separation may choose not to explore the legacy. Perhaps they contend that the loss and the grief reactions they feel are unexceptional. Some may eschew the possibility of taking actions to understand and address the impact of family separation, because they believe that to do so could threaten their equilibrium. Such people often deny the impact of adoption upon their lives and remain stuck in the separation phase. They do not display a willingness to explore why they feel as they do.

Other people choose to challenge the status quo and to take action to comprehend and address their reactions. They opt to pursue search and recovery. In my opinion, it is these people, intent upon integrating their adoption experiences into their lives, who provide themselves with the opportunity to achieve personal growth. Such persons acknowledge that an awareness of cause and effect is integral to their understanding of the effects of separation, and to achieving integration. In what follows, I examine each phase of the continuum.

Loss

Studies of the impact of separation on the family of origin have tended to focus on the birth mother and the adopted person.

However, when there is an adoption, a family disintegrates. A child is removed from both their birth parents and losses occur. The birth parents lose the child to whom they are genetically connected. They lose the opportunity to raise the child, to fulfil the traditional parenting roles. The birth mother and the birth father may also lose one another, if, prior to the adoption, they enjoyed a meaningful relationship. (Interpersonal matters for birth parents are explored in the next chapter.)

Adopted persons lose their birth parents, ties with extended family, genealogical continuity and everyday evidence of their heritage. The bond between mother and child is broken when the child is placed with adoptive parents, who offer a less fundamental connection. This is expressed neatly by Sally Howard, who notes that "In families kept intact, bonding happens and so does attachment. In [adoptive families] this is not the case because there can only be an attachment" (2003, p127).

An adopted person may not remember the original separation cognitively, but experience at a deeper level what Verrier calls "an aching sense of loss ... about which there are no conscious thoughts, only feelings and somatic memories" (1993, p27). Howard likens the separation from her birth mother to an amputation (2003, p127). In the aftermath of the separation from their birth parents, adopted persons suffer another loss – the absence of a biological connection with their adoptive parents.

For adopted persons and birth parents alike, loss may raise questions about identity. The birth mother and the birth father may rue the forced separation of the traditionally joined progenitor and child rearing roles and on the basis of a partial fulfillment only, question their right to parent subsequent children. The use of 'mother' and 'father' may cause each birth parent to ponder what these terms mean – they may equate them with loss and confusion. Adopted persons face the eternal identity quandary, which is reinforced by their dual birth certificates. The baby boy born, for example, Peter Simon, becomes, at the stroke of a pen, a person known to his adoptive parents as James Michael. No wonder many adopted persons ask, "Who am I?"!

Brodzinsky *et al* (1993, pp74–76) compare the three common causes of loss in childhood – death, divorce and adoption. Whilst there are many similarities, there are also significant differences. With death, the departed person cannot return. After a divorce, the separated parent and child often maintain contact. In the case of a closed adoption, an adopted person and their birth parents are estranged, but the loss retains an unclosed quality. The adopted person may fantasise that the situation is reversible, for the birth parents are still alive. For the same reason, birth parents may contemplate the re-appearance of their child. Because an adopted person has no history of a relationship with the birth parents, the birth mother and the birth

The Invisible Men of Adoption

father often linger as ghosts, making the loss difficult to rationalise. At the core, an adopted person has lost not only two birth parents, but also genetic connections with grandparents, siblings, aunts and uncles and cousins. In losing their genealogical and cultural linkages, they have also lost a part of themselves, which is reinforced by the acquisition of an adoptive name that replaces the name bestowed upon them by the birth parents. Because the losses experienced by an adopted person are rarely recognised by the community, there are few rituals or support systems in place to help the child deal with the consequences of the initial separation.

Two weeks after the December 2004 tsunamis devastated the coastal regions of several countries bordering the Indian Ocean, an article about loss appeared in *The Age*. The writer, Peter Ellingsen, highlights the difficulties friends and relatives experience dealing with the unknown. "It produces an awful emptiness. There's a possibility of finding him alive, or dead, or not at all," says one of the persons affected. This quotation mirrors what a member of a birth family might say. Ellingsen concludes that in the situation described, this response is to be anticipated: "... loss is what is perceived, not what in fact happens." A missing person "can trigger all the instinctive behaviours associated with grieving."

Verrier discusses the two ways in which adopted persons typically deal with loss. She characterises the behaviour of the acting-out adopted child as a distancing in an "externalised, overt, provocative manner", whilst the compliant adopted child deals with his recurring fear of abandonment by "distancing in an internalized, withdrawn, acquiescent manner" (2003, p154). As Verrier (1993) points out, these are strategies to cope with the initial loss and the potential for further losses. Neither person is exhibiting their true grieving personality for fear that if this was exhibited, it might not be appreciated by himself or significant others.

Van Keppel *et al* (1987, p4) record that, for birth mothers, their "sense of loss is typically strong and long-lasting", an observation that parallels a finding of the 1984 study by Winkler and van Keppel, which showed that approximately 50 per cent of a group of birth mothers studied reported an increase in their feelings of loss over time. Van Keppel *et al* also remind us that losing a child to adoption is accompanied by, for the birth mother, other losses, such as support, self-esteem, income and independence. As noted by van Keppel *et al*, "relinquishing a child for adoption was the most stressful life-event birth mothers had ever experienced" (1987, p3).

Clapton reports a similar finding for the birth fathers that he studied. "For many the adoption and loss of their child was a milestone or 'peak' on a graph of the emotional and psychological geography of their lives" (2003, p151). Some birth fathers may experience this as a delayed reaction emotionally, because perhaps it was their rational, practical selves that dealt with the crisis that culminated in the adoption of their child. Celia Witney (personal communication, 2003), in her study of sixty men, noted a three way loss for birth fathers – of their child, their lover and self-esteem. One birth father in Cicchini's Australian study voiced an echo of what birth mothers have found – "The feelings of loss, emptiness and helplessness have increased with every passing year" (1993, p16). Birth father Steve Davis reports in Lowe (undated) that he has "learned to live with a lot of pain and regret. Adoption isn't something that just happens and then you get on with your life. It's permanent, and it affects your life forever." Another birth father comments: "We carry these ghosts of our children in our hearts forever" (Stallings, 2004, p14). Failing to fulfil the traditional male protector/provider role may be a component of the loss that birth fathers experience.

Based on her canvassing of the views of seventy-two birth mothers, Jones (1993) observes that in the aftermath of giving up a child to adoption, the women struggled emotionally with "rage, frustration, sorrow, guilt, and self-doubt" (p7). Jones amplifies this conclusion: "Whether they'd been active or passive in the decision-making process ... all had experienced losses that they needed to address. For some, the need focussed completely on the loss of their babies. For others, it was more diffuse, including intangible losses such as the role of mother, self-esteem, or the sense of being 'good' or even 'normal' " (1993, p73). Because of the in-utero bond forged during pregnancy, a mother does not forget her child.

Grief

According to Brodzinsky *et al*, "Grieving almost always follows loss. It has many emotional and behavioral manifestations: shock, anger, depression, despair, helplessness, hopelessness. Grief can be blocked or it can be prolonged, but usually it is a normal and adaptive response to the experience of loss" (1993, p11).

When Mark Dent loses a limb to bone cancer, he reports that "The amputation of my leg was a terrible loss. I still grieve deeply for my faithful right leg" (1997, p96).

Evelyn Robinson provides an adoption setting for the conjunction between loss and grief. "You cannot have adoption without loss. Grief is not only the *expected* response to a loss, but it is also a **positive and beneficial** response, because grieving allows us to process our loss" (2001b, p2) [emphases in the reference]. The cause and effect connections are clear. An adoption results in loss, of which grief is the anticipated outcome.

Russell provides a grief framework for those with adoption experiences. "Grieving in adoption is different in some distinct ways from mourning the death of someone who has died. When someone dies, there is a definite ending that allows the grieving to begin. In adoption, there is no death, no ending. In adoption, a state of limbo exists that is similar to the dynamics of mourning someone who is missing in action. Not knowing where the person is or if they are alive blocks the grieving process. It is difficult to mourn someone who is alive but unavailable" (1996, pp46–47).

As Robinson (2003) identifies, there are often other, externally imposed impediments to grieving, which are embraced by the term 'disenfranchisement'. Disenfranchised grief translates into the relationship, the loss and the griever not being recognised by the community. As Robinson (2002) points out, "the grief of mothers who have lost children in this way is usually suppressed. Many mothers state that they did not feel that they were entitled to grieve the loss of their children ... there were no rituals and there was no gathering of the community to comfort them at the time of separation from their children" (p58). In the same article, about post-adoption grief counselling for birth mothers, Robinson acknowledges that "a number of women had been led to believe that grieving for the loss of their child was itself a sign of inadequacy on their part, making them reluctant to admit to their ongoing pain" (*ibid*). This, Robinson (2001a) observes, has consequences for birth mothers. "They usually have difficulty dealing with subsequent losses, because they did not learn how to grieve productively in what for most of them was the first major loss in their lives ..." (p3). Silverman refers to the deep seated grief of birth mothers "inasmuch as so many of them describe themselves as having been in a deep freeze, sometimes for years" (1981, p66). She acknowledges that many birth mothers have probably grieved, unknowingly, for decades.

Clapton concludes that the thirty birth fathers in his study reported suffering "feelings, behaviours and experiences" that had "parallels with what birth mothers may go through: a pathological grief reaction born of a sense of loss" (2003, p119). He reinforces how the loss is different from a typical bereavement: "In adoption the child is 'lost' yet lives on", an experience without a point of reference in the community. Clapton highlights further similarities with the reactions of birth mothers – the feelings of distress and powerlessness, as well as the persistence of the feelings of grief over a long period (2003, p119 and p206).

For adopted persons, Verrier observes, the grief experienced by a child who is separated from his birth mother has seldom been acknowledged. "It has been assumed that any deprivation which might have occurred could be overcome by the adoptive parents" (1993, p39). However, according to Robinson,

The Invisible Men of Adoption

> "... in recent years has come the realisation that adopted people, regardless of how apparently problem-free their adoptions have been, experience a deep and painful sense of loss because they have been separated from their natural mothers. Their grief resulting from this loss is not always obvious because it has usually been suppressed and is often exhibited indirectly in the behaviour of adopted people, especially in the adolescent years ... Adopted people, like their natural mothers, have not been encouraged by society to express their grief, as the expectation was that they would be grateful to their adoptive parents for 'rescuing' them. Society has traditionally admired adoptive parents for doing what appeared to be a community service by adopting children who were thought to be without families. In fact, these children did have families and they suffered from having spent their lives separated from them" (2003, pp112–113).

Robinson then draws parallels between the disenfranchised grief experienced by adopted persons and their mothers.

> "Adopted people, like natural mothers, lack a concrete focus for their grief, as they usually have no conscious memory of their natural mothers. There is also no finality to their grief, as they know that they have other families somewhere and that they will always, in some way, be a part of these families. Adopted people lack any rituals to facilitate their grieving, as they were not intellectually aware at the time that the adoption took place ... Like their natural mothers, they have often not expressed their true feelings of loss and so too often the assumption has been made that those feelings did not exist. As their natural mothers appeared to 'get on with their lives' and often showed no outward signs of their inner turmoil, so adopted people often appear to be content with their lot and show no obvious signs of grieving" (2003, p114).

The Invisible Men of Adoption

Robinson concludes that adopted people "grieve for the loss of their mothers and their natural families and that this grief affects their feelings of self-worth ..." (2003, p122).

When Zara Phillips meets her birth mother, she realises through her pain that the loss of her primary caregiver has left a legacy of unresolved grief (2004, p88). Griffith asserts that unresolved grief is at the core of the many tensions that adopted persons experience, which social workers and others find difficult to penetrate – "I believe the high degree of frustration often experienced in getting adopted persons to fully work through key issues such as rejection, anger, suppression of feelings, denial and identity conflicts, is often the failure to recognise the underlying grief" (personal communication, 2004). Griffith's observation is a further acknowledgment of the complexity of grief reactions.

Dent (1997) is a person without an adoption experience, who can provide guidance for those suffering from grief. Noting a propensity for the public to assume that a person who displays sorrow many years after experiencing a loss "has stopped living, creating and looking forward in their own life" (p115), he asserts, that to the contrary, he is living a full life, facilitated by a commitment to continue to process the loss of his leg. "I will never ignore my grief. I will never belittle or trivialise my feelings. If I feel deep hurt, I will acknowledge it, knowing that it will pass for a time but also aware that it will return, perhaps less painfully, some time in the future ... I refuse to bottle up the [emotional] pain – that is pointless ..." (Dent, 1997, p99).

In Figure 3, I have acknowledged that grief is the fundamental manifestation of loss. Individuals express their grief in various ways. Beyond profound sorrow, grieving behaviours include denial, anger, guilt, shame and various fears. Each is explored below.

The Invisible Men of Adoption

Denial

Denial may be used to block the processing of grief and become an impediment to the initiation of change. It may be a barrier to the acknowledgment of guilt and reinforce the fear of intimacy and/or rejection. Because denial represents a reluctance to face the truth, it is the most debilitating of the grief reactions, in that it represents avoidance and a static position. If feelings are suppressed deliberately, then the scope for the affected individual to recognise the multiple consequences of loss is severely compromised.

Denial is a defence strategy practised by adoptive and birth parents, as well as adopted persons. For example, adoptive parents may prefer not to remind themselves that it was infertility that caused them to consider adopting children, so that they could have a family. As a strategy to manage the emotional pain, a birth mother may deliberately or subconsciously block out any recollection of the birth of her adopted child or the signing of the consent papers that sanctioned relinquishment. For adopted persons, denial may be manifested by an unwillingness to accept that they were raised in a 'different' family, which lacked consanguinity. In some instances, the divergence is exaggerated by skin colour or a significant age gap between caregiver and child. This inability to accept reality may extend to a refusal to admit to any curiosity about their origins, because they choose to believe that the parents who guided their upbringing are the only mother and father who matter, those to whom they display allegiance. If, an adopted person's need to know about their origins goes unacknowledged by the adoptive parents, then, because an essential part of their self has been suppressed, the representation of the part of themselves which has been denied, *ie* the birth parents, may be perceived as a threat to personal equilibrium. In other circumstances, an adopted person may purposely quash their curiosity, because they fear that to explore their heritage may reveal unpleasant facts, perhaps even the presence of 'bad blood'. I know of one extreme situation, where the adopted person, an adult in his mid-thirties, denies that heritage is about bloodline. He is adamant that when he was adopted, he received the history of his adoptive parents – that their antecedents are genuinely his!

According to Russell, "Many adoptees would be too overwhelmed by the reality of their situation if they experienced clarity. Instead, living with fogginess feels comforting and protective. To have clarity is a challenge for many people. For adoptees, certain feelings may be too intense to confront" (1996, p75). Because adoption can be viewed as a life stressor, conclude Brodzinsky et al (1993), "A good many adoptees consider the stress of adoption to be something they cannot change and would be better off ignoring so they can get on with their own lives. These people reveal little inner turmoil about being adopted; they have either suppressed or denied or minimized the significance of adoption in their lives" (p151).

An adopted person's lack of curiosity about their origins can have a profound flow-on effect, as it dishonours the two persons, the birth parents, who gave them life and an identity. Similarly, those birth parents who deny wanting to know how the child they were separated from is faring, disavow their son or daughter. In both circumstances, denial is used selfishly as a tool not only to block reunion, but also to arrest the emotional development and personal growth of at least three lives.

For me, as a birth father, my denial manifested itself with a lack of willingness to confront my role in the placement of my son for adoption. The fortress I had constructed about myself for 25 years did however have a few cracks, for I experienced bouts of anger directed against objects (not people), accompanied by a guilt that, in the past, I had wronged persons I cared about. For too long, I refused to allow my denial substance and exposure. Likewise, birth father Jim Shinn recalls that after the adoption of his son, "I entered into a period of a lot of denial" (Blau, 1993, p124).

Jones (1993) reports that after the loss of their child, "Many birthmothers ... completely banished their feelings and unwittingly blocked themselves from completing the grieving process. By burying rather than experiencing their anger and [sorrow], they became stuck in denial" (p81). Jones notes further that many birth mothers internalised the judgments of their families and society. One mother, Alexis, unable to acknowledge her feelings of loss, instead dismissed them, because, at first she believed them to be 'wrong' and later because she had begun to deny them altogether (pp79–80). "Eventually, despite her deliberate suppression and conscious denial of her feelings, Alexis became debilitated by inexplicable bouts of depression and anger" (p80). I suggest that in this quotation, 'despite' could be replaced by 'because of', to reflect an actual cause and effect connection.

Anderson (1982) cautions against denial: "Attempting to suppress the most profound experience of her life separates the birthmother from herself as well as from her child, and is not healthy for anyone. It requires a great deal of emotional energy to deny or numb feelings, which limits emotional growth in all areas."

Anger

This reaction is not one of the Seven Core Issues identified by Kaplan and Silverstein. However, often it is recorded as a consequence of adoption and loss, and on this basis, I believe that it deserves to be included.

The emotion of anger, used wisely, can protect us from hurt and exploitation. However, if misused, it is no longer an ally, but a problem and a hindrance. According to Russell, "Anger is an emotion that naturally occurs when there is a loss or a feeling of being out of control. Anger can also motivate people to actions such as searching for their child or fighting for adoption reform" (1996, p85).

Evelyn Robinson, in an article entitled *Some thoughts on anger*, relates her personal experience.

The Invisible Men of Adoption

> "I spent my pregnancy being angry that I suddenly had this huge responsibility to deal with on my own. I was angry at all the people who turned their backs on me but I was also angry with all the people who thought they were being helpful because I knew that actually none of them could help me. Most of all I was angry on behalf of my child because he was not welcomed into the world with joy the way he should have been; and after my child was gone I was angry with myself for letting him go. Over the years as I thought about him growing up, I was angry at his adoptive parents because they were sharing his childhood and his development and I was not. I was angry too that while many had encouraged me to give him up for adoption, now there were also many people making me feel ashamed of my decision" (2000b, p10)

To help others, Robinson then puts her anger into context.

> "The important thing to realise is, that if you feel this way too, it's not surprising and it's nothing to apologise for ... It would be very strange if we didn't feel this rage and it would be unhealthy for us to repress it. We need to be careful, however, what we do with it ... It's natural for us to feel anger and it's fine to express our anger in a safe environment ... It's not fine, in my opinion, for us to direct our anger towards others, who were, like us, acting the way society expected them to act. We were all taken in by the myths that existed at the time; not only us but also our parents, our social workers and our children's adoptive parents" (2000b, pp10–11).

Robinson advocates that we process our anger, so that "When we begin to understand why we behaved the way we did and why those other people behaved the way they did, we may find that our anger has already subsided to some degree. We may find that we have then a sense of energy rather than rage and a desire to spread enlightenment and teach the community about our experiences" (2000b, p11). Robinson summarises her views, *viz* "Anger can be a positive and productive emotion. Bitterness is negative and destructive" (2001a, p1). Mary Murray (2002) describes how her initial (productive) reaction of anger precipitated the search for her son, a reinforcement of the benefits of a positive approach.

Verrier warns us that if anger "is inappropriate, it will stimulate aggression, which is an attempt to control or intimidate others. Or it can lead to passivity, which is another form of control, controlling by what one *doesn't* do" (1993, p192) [emphasis in the original].

Lifton notes that for adopted persons, there may be "the unexpressed anger that they are adopted; anger that they are different; anger that they are powerless to know their origins; anger that they cannot express their real feelings in a family climate of denial" (1994, p90). An adopted person may be angry at the birth parents, particularly the primary caregiver, his mother, for, he believes, giving him away. He may also be angry at the adoptive parents for replacing the birth parents. Zara Phillips feels anger towards both her birth mother and her adoptive parents, people who "had planned my future without consulting me" (2004, p63).

Verrier concludes that "adopted persons often turn their rage at the unspeakable thing that happened to them on their [adoptive parents]. Although some reunited adopted persons speak of feeling rage for their birth mothers or for the society which caused their separation from her, many will say that they feel no ill-will toward her, but have all their lives exhibited oppositional behaviour and intense rage toward their adoptive parents. Paradoxically, they feel a tremendous dependency upon and need to connect to those same adoptive parents" (1993, pp72–73).

Brodzinsky *et al* (1993, pp156–157) provide another example where anger may surface – the belated revelation in an adoptive family, often when the adopted person is a mature adult, that she is not genetically linked to the persons who raised her. Here the anger may be heightened by the years of information suppression and in some cases, deliberate lies. The anger that these adopted persons feel is often not about the circumstances of their conception and the family arrangements made on their behalf, but rather the withholding of vital information by the parents who have raised them.

I believe that the anger experienced by birth parents and adopted persons can be addressed productively. Through exploring the circumstances of the adoption, in the context of the then prevailing social environment, birth parents may fathom the actions taken by others on their behalf, against a background of community ignorance. For an adopted person, his exploration of the setting in which the adoption took place may assist him to divert his venom away from the birth parents or the adoptive parents and instead focus his misgivings more productively upon comprehending society's attitudes at the time of his placement.

Shame and Guilt

Shame and guilt are sometimes used interchangeably. However, as several writers have pointed out, there is a fundamental difference between the two. Schooler records that "[He] feels guilty for something he has done, and he feels shame for being the type of person who would have done it" (1995, p20).

Verrier reinforces the distinction in this way: "We feel guilty for what we did or imagined that we did; we feel shameful for who we are. It is the difference between *doing* and *being*" (1993, p191) [emphasis in the original]. She continues: "Shame serves no useful purpose because it cannot be integrated. It tells us that we are not worthy. It lowers our self-esteem and sabotages our sense of Self" (*ibid*). Shame is related to how we feel about ourselves; it is linked to our identity. According to Verrier, shame "is the judgment or belief that many adoptees have about themselves because they were given up for adoption" (*ibid*). This may manifest itself in a belief that they were deficient and not worthy of keeping. Verrier goes on: "If a birth mother feels shame, it is probably from some early belief about herself, not because of the relinquishment. Relinquishment is an act, which may lead to guilt" (*ibid*).

Verrier explores the nature of guilt. Asserting that it is a "judgment against ourselves", she concludes that guilt "comes in two varieties. Justifiable guilt is what one experiences when one has harmed another person or engaged in unethical conduct ... When that happens we can make amends and try to avoid repeating the offense ... Neurotic guilt, on the other hand, is guilt about something over which we had no control. It leads to blame, not accountability" (1993, pp190–191). With justifiable guilt, restitution is possible; its admission can be integrated into our lives. Neurotic guilt, however causes conflict and confusion and cannot be resolved. It is often "a cover-up for other feelings such as sorrow or anger" (Verrier, 1993, p191).

Schooler evaluates what shame and guilt mean for an adopted person. Within an adoptive family, a "source of shame for many adopted adults is the feeling that they never were what their adoptive parents had hoped for. They never measured up to the child their parents could not conceive" (1995, p19). Guilt, however, is rooted "in feeling that even as a small child she or he caused the break-up of the relationship within the birth family" (*ibid*). When a female adopted person becomes a mother herself, she may feel, as did Zara Phillips, "guilty for being able to have a baby so easily", because her adoptive mother "had never been able to have the experience of her own child" (2004, p123).

For birth parents, guilt may be the most potent representation of grief and as a result, the most difficult to address. Russell notes that for a birth mother, there "can be guilt about having sex, guilt about getting pregnant, and guilt about deciding on adoption" (1996, p84). There is also the shame and the guilt associated with pleasing others. Birth mother Amy in Jones (1993) explains: "I felt it was wrong to be pregnant and even worse to be sad about it ... I tried to ... act 'normal' to please my parents ... I was ashamed both that I was pregnant and that I *wanted* to be. I'd always been a 'good girl' and I needed to feel that I deserved that title again. But to be a 'good girl' again, my parents said I'd have to do the 'right' thing and give up my baby" (pp18–19) [emphasis in the reference]. For many birth mothers this raises the eternal core dilemma – how could relinquishment be considered both a noble sacrifice and an unmotherly act, for what 'real mother' would give up her child, despite the pressure applied to her to do so? Jones also notes that after they lost their children to adoption many birth mothers, without the support of families and others, "saw themselves as 'bad', 'undeserving of love', 'not worthy' of raising their own children ... for shaming their families, and, most of all, for relinquishing their babies" (1993, p98). Sometimes, for those who influenced the birth mother to give up her child, the guilt may surface decades later, as discovered by Sue (referring to her mother) in Jones, *viz*: "She has felt guilty, all these years, about making me surrender [my son]" (1993, p257).

Pace (2004b), referring to the ingrained shame of 'unwed' motherhood, comments about how difficult this burden is to put aside. "Few of us were allowed by parents or circumstances the choice of raising our children. Yet we were stereotyped as those very few mothers who might not have wanted their children, and who abandoned them." Anderson (1982), noting that the birth mother was absent during the celebration of the milestones in her child's life, observes that "she may feel guilty she was not there." She offers an additional reaction: "She may feel cheated she was not allowed to be there," and concludes, "either way, the loss is both painful and unnatural." Anderson concludes that, for birth mothers, there are other guilt triggers. For example, "If your (the adopted person's) adoption was not the best, she may feel guilty that she did not protect you from whatever happened and she may therefore feel she failed as a mother and as a woman. If you were raised in an abusive, neglectful, or unloving adoptive home, your birthmother may hurt for you and feel that your pain was her fault" (*ibid*).

Cicchini (1993), in his analysis of the experiences of thirty Australian birth fathers, concluded that 67% of the men studied felt guilty about the relinquishment of their child (p12) and that a similar number (61%) had felt a need to assuage that guilt by searching for their now adult child (p19). One of the birth fathers in Cicchini's study remarks: "I've carried a lot of guilt and shame about [the relinquishment of my child], and a fear of ... being found out by other people" (1993, p12). Another highlights the frequently mentioned shame-based dilemma for birth parents, when he says, "I don't tell people I have fathered three children (one adopted)" (p13). For some birth fathers, their guilt centres on ineptness and regret. "The men associated ... feelings of guilt with having not 'stood up' for themselves (and for the birth mother and the child), with not having done enough to prevent the adoption and, for those who agreed with the adoption (with hindsight perhaps) a belief that they had done something wrong" (Clapton, 2003, p137). As Clapton notes, against a background of the changing expectations of fatherhood, "fathers may have been reluctant in the past to admit to too much involvement in child care and domestic activities; now they may be reluctant to admit too little" (2003, p67) – the birth father's reaction may be a guilt-ridden silence. Mason (1995) observes that disempowerment and feelings of emotional and physical disconnectedness may trigger feelings of shame or failure; birth fathers can retain images of what could (or should) have been. Retrospective castigation may be particularly severe for those birth fathers who view their past misdeeds against the present notions of fatherhood.

It might be assumed that birth fathers who did not know of their paternity would be spared the burden of guilt. However, there is experiential evidence that birth fathers who are informed of their paternity many years after the event, begin, in some cases from the moment of revelation, to feel guilty about the prolonged absence from their child's life.

Fear

There are a number of reactions to loss that I have gathered under the heading of 'Fear'. Each represents at best an anxiety, at worst a dread. Because the fears of intimacy or being rejected or controlled by others have relationships at their core, they may take considerable courage and effort to overcome.

Intimacy

Birth parents and adopted persons alike report that the intimacy which culminated in an adoption often leaves a legacy of distrust and impaired self-esteem.

Kaplan and Silverstein conclude that "people who have had significant losses in their lives may fear getting close to others because of the risk of experiencing loss again" (1991, Section 2, p3). They continue: "Birthparents may connect the loss of their child with the sexual encounter that led to the pregnancy, and fear intimacy because they believe it leads to loss" (*ibid*).

Jones (1993) reports that many of the women in her study felt that their ability to relate to others was compromised after they were separated from their children. "Most agreed that their problems with intimacy were not limited to marriages or relationships with men but extended to friendships with women and interactions with their parents and siblings as well ... Those whose trust and self-confidence had been casualties of relinquishing felt that, without these qualities, their subsequent relationships were, from the start, destined to be impaired" (p139).

Jones noted that nine out of ten women she interviewed about post-adoption relationships married within two years of losing their child to adoption. A significant number thought that they had married for the wrong reasons or married the wrong man. For some, social acceptability to escape the stigma of losing a child was the incentive to marry soon after the adoption was finalised. Often, these marriages were loveless, which, as Jones points out, "seemed the most plausible and effective defense against the potential pain of intimacy" (1993, p120). Some birth mothers feel so threatened by the risks of close relationships that they isolate themselves from other people for months, even years,

The Invisible Men of Adoption

choosing in some cases, never to marry, or to pursue an alternative commitment to a career. Among those who consciously avoided men because "intimacy would only mean further pain ... some went out of their way to avoid attracting the opposite sex" (Jones, 1993, p134). Sue, one of the women interviewed by Jones, convinced herself that love had been the root cause of her post-relinquishment despair. "As a result, I became afraid of my sexuality ... I became frigid towards men" (p92).

These overall sentiments are to some degree echoed by birth fathers. Men in Cicchini's 1993 study report that: "I just can't start a good relationship with a woman. As soon as they get too close I walk away" (p12), "I am finding difficulty forming a lasting meaningful relationship" (p13) and "I drifted from one 'permanent' relationship to the next" (p9). One of the men in Clapton's study of birth fathers concludes that his failure to commit to a partner is affected by caution, which is related to his negative experience of adoption (2003, p145). "Others believed that the adoption experience had influenced their general attitude to all relationships" and "their negative attitudes originated in the experience of loss and disenfranchisement during the adoption" (Clapton, 2003, p147).

According to Verrier (1993), "Many adoptees find it difficult to attach or allow closeness in relationships because of the fear that each new relationship, *like the very first relationship*, will not last" (p90) [emphasis in the original]. Because of this same fear, "Separating seems an even greater problem than attaching. Once a relationship is established many adoptees do not want to separate, even when the relationship proves unsatisfactory" (*ibid*). Simultaneous conflicting desires for merger and independence can create relationship complications for some adopted persons. "The fear of abandonment often keeps an adoptee from getting close to those with whom he is in relationship. When he begins to feel connected to another person, he will do something to distance himself from his partner and find a sense of safety again" (Verrier, 2003, p217). Lifton points out that, for adopted persons who have constructed protective mechanisms to disguise their real feelings, they "often avoid intimacy for fear of being discovered for the impostors they know they are. Let down your guard, they think, and everyone will see that under the confident self you present to the world, there is really a weak and frightened child. Better to keep your distance to avoid being abandoned again" (1994, p115).

Rejection

More so than the other fears, rejection may be an unfounded perception and, as such, have the potential to cause the greatest harm, if not assessed objectively. Fundamentally, rejection is a projection of how we fear others may react to us.

Kaplan and Silverstein maintain that "Adoptees often feel they were placed for adoption because they were worthless or defective ... Some may take responsibility for being rejected, believing they did something to cause it" (1991, Section 2, p1). Some link the adoption to the assumption that to be available for their adoptive parents, they had first to be 'given up' by their birth parents. For an adopted person, the ultimate fear, should they initiate the quest for reunion, may be that their birth parents will reject them a second time. Should this potential setback be averted, the possibility that unless they are on their best behaviour, reunion will be terminated by the birth parent, still lurks in the background.

Russell points out that "Some adoptees protect themselves from the threat of rejection ... by rejecting others before they can be rejected ... For [some] adoptees, the fear of ... rejection is never far away and can interfere with getting close to people" (1996, p69). Schooler concurs, by saying of adopted persons that "Their perceptions of rejection can spill over to affect the building of healthy relationships" (1995, p18). On the same theme Kaplan and Silverstein observe that "Not only can feelings of rejection lead to impaired self-esteem [but] adoptees may anticipate rejection and either set themselves up for it in their relationships or try to please others so they are not rejected" (1991, Section 2, p2). Verrier (2003, p56) explores the impact of these perceptions, by noting the propensity of many adopted persons to interpret observations as personal criticisms and disagreements with their viewpoint as rejection. These can be personal 'landmines' for adopted persons. Verrier discusses the eternal dilemma for adopted persons. "If someone rejects the outside you, that's not so bad, because it isn't really you; but if you let someone know who you really are inside and they reject you, that's *really* rejection. The 'false' self is the adoptees' method of adjusting to their environment in order to protect themselves from further ... rejection" (1993, p35) [emphasis in the original]. Verrier observes that, in adulthood, adoptees are like chameleons. "They are very good at adapting, because they spent their childhood perfecting the art of adapting to their adoptive families", so avoiding being rejected by their caregivers (2003, p50).

For an adopted person, the fear of rejection may be linked to the original separation. At the time, the infant may internalise the original separation as abandonment, for the fundamental mother–child bond was broken. An adopted person, as a child, an adolescent and an adult may prepare and use strategies that externalise their fear of rejection by others. Phillips observes: "I didn't want to hurt my [adoptive] mother by asking too many questions, so I began to protect my family from my real feelings ... I didn't want to be rejected" (2004, p22). Robinson also comments about the suppression of feelings as a preservation mechanism: "Many adopted persons are cautious and fear abandonment. As a result, they tend to be undemonstrative and to avoid commitment. This is their way of protecting themselves against what they might perceive as a rejection" (2009, p64).

Of birth parents, Kaplan and Silverstein comment "[they] may reject themselves as irresponsible or unworthy to be a parent. They often keep the fact that they placed a child for adoption a secret because they fear people would reject them if they knew the truth" (1991, Section 2, p2).

The Invisible Men of Adoption

It is not uncommon for birth parents to be accused of abandoning their child. Most renounce the proposition, that in losing their child through adoption, they rejected and continue to reject their progeny. To them, there is a world of difference between not wanting to keep a child and being unable to keep a child. This is expressed by Robinson: "I have never yet heard a mother or father say that in allowing their child to be adopted, they were rejecting or abandoning that child" (2004, p161). Personal, often heart-rending narratives by birth parents are filled with the pain of the separation itself and the consequences of living apart from consanguineous family members. Embedded in this hurt and grief is the concern that actions, which resulted in the estrangement of parent and child, may be misinterpreted as abandonment and rejection. As noted by Robinson, "some people interpret the other person's behaviour as rejection or abandonment, but people rarely describe their own behaviour in that way" (2004, p219). Robinson points out that if birth parents had had any idea that their actions would cause their children to perceive they had been abandoned, "they would have had more reason to resist the idea of adoption. Many of them did not resist, because they were told that by allowing their children to be adopted, they were actually doing them a great favour and showing how much they cared about their well-being" (2004, p8).

Despite these assurances, birth parents may still be haunted by the spectre of rejection by their son or daughter. Whilst they have rationalised their own actions, they cannot vouch for their child's perceptions. In the face of contrary evidence, they may fear that the adult child can never forgive his mother and father for giving him away. For many birth parents, their greatest fear is that their child will not want to know them. Whether the birth parent is the one sought by the adopted person or the person initiating the search, this fear can become overwhelming.

For those birth parents who have not told their spouse, siblings, later children or parents of the presence of an adopted child, there is the spectre of rejection, should they reveal the secret to family members after an interval of many years. Other birth mothers and birth fathers may have to re-write the script and correct the misinformation they had offered previously. Because of this turnaround, they may fear renunciation.

Anderson (1982) presents another viewpoint, presented from the perspective of an adopted adult: "If she (the birth mother) believes your (the child's) adoption was best for you, she may feel worthless or useless as a mother because you did not need her, and thus feel she is a failure as a mother and a woman. If you are glad your adoptive parents instead of your birthmother raised you, your birthmother may feel rejected or unimportant to you. This causes her pain. A good adoptive home can reinforce her feelings of inadequacy and of being 'not good enough' to be your mother."

Control

As humans, we prefer to exercise control over our lives, rather than have others impose their will upon us. Often, those people with adoption experiences speak of being disempowered, of having decisions made for them rather than by them. The original parent–child separation is the critical moment for the birth mother, the birth father and their son or daughter. The adoption may leave a legacy of wariness for all members of the family of origin and a resolve to avoid manipulation by others, thereafter. However, this goal may prove elusive.

In the United Kingdom, it has been common for social workers acting on behalf of birth parents to approach adult adopted persons via the adoptive parents. This strategy has serious ramifications. Adopted persons are treated as perpetual children. Birth parents can be reminded of events surrounding the adoption, a former occasion when they felt disempowered. Adoptive parents, acting as messengers on behalf of the children they have raised, may assume the role of power-brokers and keep news of the proposed outreach to themselves, thereby blocking or, at best, postponing a reunion. In the above scenario, the intended reunion participants have relinquished control to social workers and/or adoptive parents, persons who may not have the best interests of the searcher and the person sought at heart.

According to Verrier, "One of the ways in which children (and adults, too) try to prevent future losses is to try to be in absolute control of every situation" (1993, p78). For adopted persons the fear of not being in control is paramount. *"The child was not in control of the situation at the beginning of his life, and look what happened!* It becomes intolerable to these children ever again to allow anyone else to be in control of their lives" (Verrier, 1993, p79) [emphasis in the original]. Many adopted persons develop strategies to maintain control. "Having been manipulated at the beginning of their lives makes some adoptees manipulative and controlling ... Some adoptees control situations by becoming isolated and detached, while others are more overt in their controlling mechanisms" (Verrier, 1993, p97). In her second book, Verrier cautions adopted persons. "Even as you ensure that you are not being controlled by that other person, *you are not in control* ... You are being controlled instead by your own fear of being controlled – by the little scared child inside, who is still in the grips of the fear of that first loss" (2003, p201) [emphasis in the original].

Jones (1993) observes that "No mother in the world, human or animal, would *decide* to give up her baby. It isn't normal or natural. It wouldn't happen if mothers had the power to decide [*ie* be in control]. It only happens when they don't" (p12) [emphasis in the reference]. She records that of the birth mothers interviewed in her study, "most ... relinquished not because they wanted to, but because their pregnancies broke the rules, opposed social standards, and threatened to leave them forever isolated from respectable society" (p13). In the aftermath of the adoption, "Birthmothers ... often began patterns of strict emotional control that they maintained for years ... [They] tried to control their relationships ... Having lacked control over their babies, they were determined to maintain tight reins over the remainder of their lives, often defying authority or rejecting both people and opportunities that represented risk" (Jones, 1993, p99). These women systematically avoided situations in which they again might feel powerless.

Disempowerment is a common reaction reported by birth fathers. The relinquishment of control before and at the time of the birth of their child, frequently to one or both sets of parents, may leave the men feeling diminished, wary because their trust has been fractured. There is evidence that some birth fathers have over-compensated in subsequent relationships for the control they forsook when their child was adopted.

A few thoughts about Trust

I have not accorded trust the status of a separate entity, principally because its effects are diverse.

Trust cements relationships. For an adopted person, trust may be destroyed by the original mother–child separation. According to PARC, if a mother is "consistent, loving and responsive" in meeting the needs of her baby, then the infant comes to trust her, and attachment develops (2004, p7). Having lost her birth mother, "every adopted child comes to her new family with attachment problems" (*ibid*). As described by Verrier, "The loss of the mother disallows the achievement of basic trust, the first milestone in the healthy development of a human being" (1993, p36). The development of trust is an essential component of identity. It allows adopted (and all) persons to believe in themselves and in others. Trust may affect intimacy; without it, lasting, loving relationships are not possible. Verrier summarises the negative impacts. "Distrust is evident, not only in the permanency of relationships, but in the goodness of self ... This lack of self-esteem or self-worth is intricately intertwined with the lack of trust and fear of intimacy described by many ... adoptees" (1993, p90).

"Many birth mothers," writes Verrier, "have lost their trust in family and professionals. From the time that their family members urged them to give up their babies for adoption, they began to distrust those relationships ... They lost trust, not only in their family members and professionals, but in their own judgment" (2003, p224). Anderson (1982) concludes that the loss of trust can have a lasting effect: "If the people [the birth mother] loved and trusted, who she thought would always love and help her, abandoned her when she most needed them, she may feel unable to trust anyone now."

According to Jones (1993), when birth mothers confronted the loss of their child, they often encountered issues of broken trust, related to the birth father, family and adoption professionals (p40). For some, the reluctance to trust extended to themselves; "they didn't trust themselves to accomplish, maintain or merit *any* goal or relationship ... Accomplishments in careers, parenting, or other efforts ... were credited to others than themselves" (p125) [emphasis in the original]. Here, the inability to have faith in themselves and to acknowledge personal achievements is rooted in feelings of self-worth, an element of identity.

Identity

Because it has at its heart what we think of ourselves, identity is a bridge that spans separation and healing. It governs how we react to loss and it affects the degree to which we recover from this misfortune.

For an adopted person, the separation of birth parent and child may result in bewilderment about their heritage. Birth parents may feel uncertain about what it means to be a mother or a father. These are issues related to how people view themselves. During the integration phase, awareness, self-responsibility and the will to advance can be employed productively by family of origin members, to help each understand what it means to be an adopted person, a birth mother or a birth father. Those who choose to be proactive often report that they feel better about themselves.

The Invisible Men of Adoption

Identity confusion

As pointed out by Brodzinsky *et al*, "The search for self is universal and ongoing ... Our sense of who we are is influenced by every experience we have; it's changed each time our life circumstances change" (1993, p13). It is not only the major events such as birth, death and marriage, and for those so affected, adoption, but also the summation of lesser happenings, such as each compliment or rejection, achievement or failure that add to how we feel about ourselves. Brodzinsky *et al* continue: "... adoptees have a particularly complex task in their search for self. When you live with your biological family, you have guideposts to help you along. You can see bits of your own future reflected in your parents, pieces of your own personality echoed in your brothers and sisters. There are fewer such clues for someone who is adopted" (*ibid*). 'Genealogical bewilderment' is a term that is sometimes used to describe this dilemma. Jayne Schooler (1995, p166) reports on further work by Brodzinsky, in which he points out that we have different identities in different contexts, *eg* an occupational identity, a religious identity, an identity as the member of a family, etc. An individual integrates these various aspects of the self, including elements related to family. For an adult adopted person, there is a complication, for they have three families – one that they know, and two, the families of the respective birth parents that they do not know.

Lifton notes that in order to survive family complexities, adopted persons assume dual identities.

> "Early on they get the message that they cannot grieve for their lost kin but must commit themselves to the identity of the adoptive clan if they are to keep the adoptive parent's love. Already abandoned by the birth mother, the child feels no choice but to abandon her, and by so doing, abandon his real self. This early potential self that is still attached to the birth mother is unacceptable to the adoptive parents and, therefore, must become unacceptable to the child ... The child forced to give up the real self cannot develop feelings of

belonging ... Adopted children often try to shut out the subject of adoption. This means that they must separate one part of the self from the rest of the self" (2002, p210).

Within the adopted child, Lifton identifies

"... the Artificial Self and the Forbidden Self, neither of which is completely true or completely false. The Artificial Self seems like the perfect child because she is so eager to please. She is compliant, puts everyone's needs before her own, and suppresses her anger. But deep inside she feels like a fake and an imposter, feelings that may overwhelm her as an adult. Having cut off a vital part of herself, she sometimes feels dead. The Forbidden Self is more difficult. Refusing to please, he becomes oppositional, often acting out antisocially as a way of feeling alive. An adoptee may switch from one self to the other during various stages of the life cycle. The perfect child may express her or his anger in adulthood. And the Forbidden Self may eventually become a dutiful son or daughter" (*ibid*).

Verrier terms these coping strategies the False Self – defence mechanisms employed by the child to deal with the loss of the part of their Self that was wounded before he or she began "to separate [their] own identity from that of [the] mother, ... leaving the infant with a feeling of incompleteness or lack of wholeness" (1993, p38).

For adopted persons, there is another layer that adds to the complexity. The issuing of a second birth certificate, which replaces the names they were given at birth with new names, teaches adopted persons that their identity can be discarded. As Robinson points out, "Giving them a 'new' (*ie* false) identity suggests to them that who they actually are is unacceptable and must be hidden" (2004, p189).

Within adopted families, not belonging may be obvious.

The Invisible Men of Adoption

> "Often an undeniable fact that an adoptee does not resemble family members stimulates intense feelings of aloneness. Steve Harris, for example, did not look anything like his family. 'I would go to family reunions and everyone was tall and thin and I was short and stocky. They had dark complexions and I was much lighter ... I would spend a week with people who were supposed to be family, but we didn't have anything in common. I looked different. My personality and temperament were different. I would come home feeling like I didn't belong' " (Hochman *et al*, 1998, p12).

Samantha, in *issues*, Number 13, of January–March 1999 speaks of a similar experience. "I used to ... get up in the morning and look at my face [in the mirror], then go and have breakfast with people that seemed to be total strangers. I guess that ... I never felt as though I really belonged. Not just because of my looks, but everything about me" (p16). Samantha then reveals the breakthrough: "At the age of 20, I found my uncle; the minute he opened the door he knew who I was." Later she meets her birth mother. "I could see physical resemblances ... the same coloured skin and hair, and the extroverted personalities ... I had found a very big part of myself to identify with" (*ibid*).

For birth parents also there is the potential for identity confusion. They are the two people who conceived the child; therefore they are the mother and the father. However, the adoptive parents who raise the child are also a mother and a father. Because they did not raise the child, some birth parents have difficulty acknowledging biological and genetic facts. In some circumstances, the confusion may have had its roots in the claim made at the time of the adoption that the adoptive parents were henceforth the 'real' parents. However, the original roles and the fundamental connections with birth parents do not disappear when the child is placed with another family. To be called 'former birth parent' is not an option.

For birth mothers, there is what is called the 'double bind', which affects their identity as a mother: " 'If you love your child you will give [him] up.' Then when they do, they are told,

'You've given [him] up, so you don't love [him] and you've no right to know anything more about [him]' " (Griffith, 1991, Section 5, p9). Judgmental persons in the community might add the comment that a birth mother's relinquishment of her baby was proof that she did deserve to be mother anyway.

Some of the birth mothers in Jones' study report trying to change their exterior, to become the 'perfect woman' to rectify their indiscretion. One, Sue, says "I was determined to make up for everything I'd done wrong. I was obsessed with trying to be a 'good girl' again, to regain my self-image" (1993, p91). Jones notes further that for many of birth mothers, as an essential part of their identity, their "self-esteem had been destroyed" by the relinquishment (p110).

Birth fathers' issues with their identity may centre on their right to call themselves a father because they did not fulfil the roles of providing for and watching over their child. They may feel that because they were not at the birth or outside the hospital, their claim to be the father is weakened.

Search and Recovery

To address the consequences of adoption, each member of the family of origin has to make a crucial change – from reacting to the parent–child separation, to taking action. If no effort is made to address the fundamental loss and grief issues, the individual risks remaining static, possibly consumed (whether recognised or not) by the responses to grief. In my opinion, this is an unacceptable risk, one, that if chosen, prevents recovery and personal growth.

Robinson applies dual meanings to 'recovery'. The first refers to healing the emotional pain caused by adoption separation, as it applies to an individual. The second aspect addresses the situation where separated members of the family of origin are reunited; they are 'recovering' the relationship that was interrupted by the adoption (2004, Introduction). Both components are displayed in Figure 3.

The self

Mending the hurt self takes courage. It requires, firstly an acknowledgment that the original separation of birth parent and adopted child has caused damage. Then, there needs to be a commitment on the part of the individual to focus on the wounds, objectively and with the intention of learning from their effects, rather than blaming others for their original infliction. These, the necessary ingredients of the 'search' phase, are the foundations for 'recovery'. For adopted persons and birth parents alike, personal healing represents, as Robinson puts it, "freeing up the energy that has been tied up in suppressing their grief ... If personal recovery work is not undertaken, then those affected by adoption separation can remain locked into denial and the anxiety which results from it" (2004, p21). The advice offered in Butler-Bowdon may assist: "The best way of overcoming fear is to be curious about that which you fear" (2001, p266).

Robinson places personal recovery on two levels. "On an intellectual level, you are aiming to understand what happened and on an emotional level, you are aiming to get in touch with how you feel about what happened" (2004, p22). For birth parents, recovery work may profitably include consideration of their family upbringing, the values that were the foundation of the family (including how much children were appreciated for their own sake), the relationship they had with their parents, how the family dealt with internal and external changes that occurred, the prevailing social attitudes, how news of the out-of-wedlock pregnancy was disclosed and received, who made the decisions that led to the adoption and whose interests was the separation of parent and child deemed to serve. It is also beneficial to explore the impact that the initial loss caused by the adoption has had on personal life afterwards, as well as the repercussions for relationships within the family and with others, the effects on self-esteem and the ability to trust other people, the consequences for decision-making and the capacity to deal with subsequent losses. An appreciation of the evolution of community attitudes towards out-of-wedlock conceptions may also be helpful. Telling your story, whether orally or in writing may assist with the release of feelings previously suppressed by disenfranchised grief. Support groups, attended by people with similar experiences, may help validate your personal narrative. Some people may choose to share more. Beyond the fruitful oral sharing, writing about my adoption experience has helped me not only to understand the influential events and their background, but also made me feel better about myself.

Healing is possible only when the consequences of the original separation and loss are acknowledged and addressed, as reinforced by Phillips, who writes: "Until I could recognize my loss and allow my grief to surface, I was incapable of developing a trusting relationship or having a healthy marriage" (2004, p154).

For adopted persons, their personal healing might usefully focus on how they reacted to discovering that they were adopted and what it was like for them to grow up in their adoptive family. It may also prove productive for them if they incorporate an investigation of the evolution of social attitudes to adoption. To aid their progression, Verrier has a general word of advice for adopted persons. She advocates "sharing yourself with those close to you" (2003, p62). However, for this communication to be effective, "It means first learning who you are, so that you can share your authentic self and not that false self you fashioned out of trauma-based behavior that at one time helped you to cope" (*ibid*). As Robinson puts it, with advice for all members of the family of origin,

> "When you have a sense that you have achieved a level of acceptance of the issues surrounding your adoption separation experience, it is likely that you will feel more comfortable

> sharing your experience with others ... If you are able to present your experience to others in a powerful and confident manner, then you will find that you no longer feel the sense of shame and guilt that you may have felt prior to undertaking personal recovery work" (2004, p38)

and

> "Whether or not a reunion takes place ... personal recovery work plays a vital role in the journey towards healing for those who have experienced an adoption separation" (*ibid*).

Anecdotal evidence suggests that few people regret undertaking personal healing, whether or not it leads to the next stage – reunion.

Parent and child reunion

For many people who have adoption experiences, personal healing provides the catalyst to seek reunion. Those who have 'gone inside' are usually well placed to advance to meeting the person from whom they were separated by adoption. These persons will have addressed the feelings associated with their loss and grief, resulting perhaps in diminished anger, guilt and sorrow, ideal personal preparation for a reunion.

From an incentive viewpoint, those who initiate searches are perhaps more likely than the recipients of outreach to have undertaken personal recovery tasks. On this basis, the searcher may enjoy an advantage. For those who are the subject of searches, the invitation to participate in reunion presents an opportunity for interpersonal recovery, which may provide a catalyst to initiate or to re-invigorate personal recovery work. Sometimes, as in the case of Evelyn Robinson and her son Stephen, individual searches, without the knowledge of the other, are concurrent (Robinson, 2003). In their case, each had performed independent personal recovery work, paving the way for mutually sought interpersonal healing.

Reunion represents a part of the quest for wholeness, or, as Lifton puts it, in the case of adopted persons, the "need for biological, historical, and human connectedness" (1994, p128). Persons separated by adoption can make significant contributions to their own well-being and that of the other party by agreeing to participate in reunion. Again, this is reinforced by Lifton, who asserts that "empowerment and reconnection are the core experiences of recovery" (1994, p128).

The healing can be viewed at two levels. Firstly, both parent and child are part of each other's identity. Every child embodies the genetic characteristics passed on by their mother and their father, whether or not they become an adopted person. The mother and the father (in the case of an adoption, the birth father and the birth mother) pass on their genes to the child. It is natural for any child separated from their parents to wish to know their heritage. As a corollary, I believe it is natural, as with any parent, for birth mothers and birth fathers to wish to meet and spend time with the person to whom they are intimately related and to whom they have bequeathed their genes. Typically, birth parents are precluded from participating in the joys of the day-to-day parenting of their adopted child. This heightened sense of having 'missed out' reinforces the birth parents' imperative to find the part of their legacy and their lives that is 'missing'. The second component is the grief caused by the original separation; reunion represents an opportunity to integrate the loss and its consequences into three lives and thus provide mending for all.

The focal point of recovery may differ for each participant. The baby who subsequently becomes an adopted person was carried by the birth mother for nine months before the birth. During this period, a bond with psychological, genetic and biological elements was established. The birth father is linked to his offspring genetically and, assuming he is aware of the presence of the child, psychologically. When an adopted child is separated from his mother and father, he is removed (at best temporarily) from his genetic markers, such as facial features, body language, talents and basic personality, facets of the gene pool provided by the birth parents. An infant, because of the bond forged during pregnancy, does know his mother and instinctively wants to be with her. It is to be expected that for adopted persons, issues surrounding their identity, including perhaps the perception that they were not good enough for their birth mother to keep, are the focus of their recovery. This fundamental quest for identity may in part explain why it is more common for adopted persons to initiate searches for their birth parents, usually the birth mother, than vice versa.

MacKay, placing her focus on the benefits of recovery, opines that "the act of searching and/or maintaining a relationship with the birth family reclaims the adoptee's autonomy, power and equality" (2005, p18). Lifton acknowledges that for adopted persons, whatever the degree of healing, "after search and reunion, at least they have a potential for growth" (1994, p272). I maintain that the same maxim applies to birth parents.

For the birth mother who has lost her baby, it is likely that the grief that results from being separated from her child will be the focal point of her pain and her healing. Her feeling of loss is immediate, acute and likely to increase over time. A birth father's responses may be more complex. His relationship with the birth mother was at the very least physical and, based on published studies, often affectional. He may never have seen his child, if his relationship with the birth mother ended before the birth, or if he was absent during the period between the birth and the adoption. His child may not have the tangible presence experienced by the birth mother. It may be years later that the separation from his child is acknowledged emotionally by the birth father, when he realises that what he has lost is the opportunity to participate daily in the life of the child he has never seen. His sense of loss may lie dormant, but when realised, become profound. Towards the birth mother he knew, a birth father's reaction is more likely to be centred on guilt, a perception that he has let her down, causing the mother–child bond to be broken. Redressing these matters may become the essence of the reconciliation and the mending he seeks with the birth mother. The birth mother's reciprocal reaction, if she feels that she was forsaken, may be anger towards the birth father.

Schooler (1995) issues a cautionary note about the expression of anger during reunion. "[The birth mother] may be angry with her family or her boyfriend (at the time) for not helping her when she needed it most. She may be angry with herself for not being stronger and standing up for what she truly wanted – to keep her child ... all that anger could manifest itself in anger toward the adoptee ... when she's really angry about what she's remembering" (p145) and "this anger is never for the person. It is an anger for a situation that was out of their control" (p143). She also refers to the release of guilt and shame: "The pressures of family, clergy, social workers and society created the belief that women who were pregnant out of marriage and surrendered their child were worthless ... Many ... are not able to get past ... the accompanying shame when found by their ... child. When contact is made by the ... child, old feelings of shame and guilt rush to the surface" (pp142–143).

In her study, Jones (1993) observes that "Many birthmothers emphasized that reunion was *not* a cure for the regrets, angers, or grief they faced after relinquishing. Reunion had, in fact, offered additional risks of rejection, disappointment, and confrontation with the events, issues, and emotions of the past" (p211) [emphasis in the reference]. The reactions of these women confirm the observation that reunions can be beset by "pain, conflict and confusion" (Anderson, 1982). "However," Anderson concludes, "reunion does not cause these difficulties, it is the unnatural separation from one's baby, one's child. The feelings already exist and leaving them buried beneath denials and fantasies cannot resolve or eliminate them" (*ibid*).

It is probable that a number of the birth mothers in Jones' study had not undertaken personal recovery work as preparation for the possibility of reunion, because outreach by their adult adopted children placed them in a position where they "were compelled to resume the grieving they'd abandoned years ago and to confront the toll relinquishing had taken on their lives" (Jones, 1993, p206). Overall, says Jones, "With reunions, risks were taken, secrets were revealed, truths were confronted" as a result of which, "Although reunions often emphasized the losses of the past, they also offered opportunities for the birthmothers and their [separated] children to salvage their futures" (1993, p229). Jones concludes that for many birth mothers, healing was possible because they allowed "themselves to grieve and mourn, to seek support and help when they need[ed] it [and] to assert themselves as individuals" (1993, p287).

Robinson (2004) "[believes] that it is appropriate for reunion between family members separated by adoption to be encouraged and promoted" (p41), She concludes that "Reunion represents the loss of ignorance and fear. Reunion can replace ignorance with knowledge and fear with confidence" (p42). Robinson then sounds a warning for those who enter reunion without preparatory work: "If ... no attempt at personal recovery has been made before the reunion event takes place, then the impact often seems to be greater, as the grief has been dormant for ... longer ... and has not already been processed, even in part. I believe that this is why many reunion experiences resemble bereavement situations and can cause major grieving behaviours to be exhibited" (2004, p50). The birth fathers in the study undertaken by Passmore and Coles (2009) who reported that the reunions with their adult children presented emotional challenges may have undertaken only limited preparatory personal recovery work.

Usually, it is impossible to know beforehand what stage the sought person has reached in their healing. It is likely that the person who initiates the reunion believes that, from their personal perspective, they are ready to meet the person from whom they were separated. However, they may encounter a person who denies that adoption separation has affected their life, or one who realises that they have many yet unresolved issues to address for themselves. Even in the circumstance where the initiator is, believing they have it 'all together', reunited with a person who has an awareness of their own separation issues, for good reasons it is likely that the reunion will raise fresh emotional issues, ones that an individual working alone cannot resolve.

Birth parents and adopted persons who address their grief through personal recovery work often face fresh challenges when reunion occurs. Because the loss precipitated by the adoption is not final, in that a death has not occurred and given that the grief experienced by the participants in the original separation is disenfranchised, healing complexities are to be expected. Unlike a death, where the mourners accept that the deceased has departed, adoption separation creates an ambiguous situation, where the possibility of members of the family of origin finding each other is ever present. Consequently, full grieving can be delayed until the 'missing' members of the family of origin are reunited. Unbidden, the reunion creates the catalyst for the pain of the initial separation to be resurrected. Many birth parents and adopted persons report being surprised by the intensity of the emotions released during their reunions. However, if both persons can acknowledge that it is the original separation that caused the grief and that reunion represents an opportunity for grief resolution, then this is sound preparation for advancement.

Robinson (2004, p61) identifies four possible reunion outcomes. There are those who successfully complete the mourning tasks and incorporate the adoption experience into their lives. There are those who enter the reunion, but choose not to perform the mourning tasks and so retain the loss and associated grief as unresolved issues. There are those who want to reach out for reunion but cannot proceed because the other person is unavailable to them, through death, a failure to be located or a refusal to participate. Finally, there is the situation where neither party is willing to enter reunion, confront their grief and accept the benefits that working together can bring. Of the four, only the first is a productive result for both parties. It signifies that both participants have recognised the benefits of openness and the potential for recovery. As anybody separated by an adoption knows, there is a likelihood of outreach, but it is the preparedness of each individual to accept the possibility of reunion and see it as an opportunity for healing and personal growth that governs their choices and determines the outcome. In the second situation above, when the parties meet, progress is compromised because the fundamental issues resulting from the initial separation are not addressed. The third and fourth scenarios involve persons who are not (yet) ready to acknowledge the missing part of themselves and the importance of the other. For those who choose not to participate in reunion, there can be long term negative consequences. The grief, whether or not acknowledged, remains a burden and a barrier to personal growth. According to Robinson (2004, p65), a person in denial may suffer physical symptoms or engage in aberrant behaviour. To suppress the pain, some may turn to drugs or alcohol, whilst others avoid person-to-person contact by relocating physically to a distant place.

The matter of trust, displayed as wariness or even jealousy, may become an issue for spouses when contact and reunion occur. Anecdotal evidence suggests that the husband or wife of an adopted person, the wife of a birth father and the husband of a birth mother may experience difficulties accepting the inclusion of the returning family of origin member into the fold. Members of families separated by an adoption have a bond based on consanguinity; the spouse is related by marriage only to the initiator or recipient of contact. It is no surprise that the spouse might feel left out, as parent and child (or in the case of birth parents re-establishing contact, mother and father) enter reunion. Carlene Wood (personal communication, 2004) offers the observation that reactions are sometimes more intense if the entrant into the family is of the same gender as the spouse, *eg* a wife may feel threatened by contact initiated by her birth father husband's daughter. However, if a spouse allows space and displays generosity towards their partner, as they address the loss and the grief issues that resulted from the original separation, this is sure to be appreciated.

The Invisible Men of Adoption

By definition, a reunion is between members of the family of origin. Other people, related either directly by marriage or through adoption, did not experience the original separation, so cannot be reunited. Friends and interested others are also observers, not participants. All these people, in particular the spouse, and in the case of adopted persons, the adoptive parents, do, however, have a critical role to play – providing unconditional support for those contemplating or engaged in reunion. Anderson has this to say about the specific contribution of adoptive parents: "When [they] ... give support and understanding, they give their children freedom, and with it the knowledge that they love and respect both their children and themselves" (1997, p9). I contend that the thrust of this statement applies also to what loving spouses can offer.

Whilst a great deal of satisfaction and inner peace can be achieved through personal healing, reunion represents an investment in restoring a lost relationship. It is a relationship that is centred on loss, but realises the benefits of 'finding' not only one's self but also the other person. It is important, however, to remind ourselves about the role of personal responsibility. We cannot ask the person from whom we were separated by adoption to be responsible for mending us, for this can be construed by them as blame for our predicament. At best, such a request is tantamount to asking the other person to own our personal issues. We are each responsible for our <u>own</u> healing, whether or not reunion takes place. If the reunion does not meet expectations, then we can choose to take what was offered and apply it to our personal recovery.

Ultimately, it is only through taking personal responsibility that those separated by adoption can achieve reunion, as well as resolve issues surrounding their self-worth.

Identity settlement

Because taking ownership of one's actions, whether or not it results in reunion, has an impact on how an individual perceives himself or herself, both personal and interpersonal recovery can have an impact on 'identity'.

Schooler (1995) records the reactions of adopted persons: "Because of our reunion, my life is richer and fuller" (p190) and "Searching felt like the biggest risk I've ever taken in my life, yet I couldn't be complete without knowing" (p191). Robinson (2004) includes a personal message from her son, in which he writes, that as a result of reunion, "I personally feel much more whole. I now have a fuller understanding of my origins and therefore of who I am." Mary Keller states "Connecting with my birth family has given me a sense of completion ... and the knowledge of my own story" (Blau, 1993, p100). These individual comments by adopted persons reinforce the conclusions reached by others. Brodzinsky *et al* note that "the consolidation of identity" is an important outcome of searching (1993, p145). Marshall and McDonald (2001, p245) record that, from an Australian study of the reunion experiences of adopted persons, identity issues, related to "the knowledge they had gained about themselves and their family background" emerged as a critical factor. Stephanie Mello, in Blau (1993) summarises the benefits of identity settlement for adopted persons – "to help [them] understand themselves better, to feel stronger and more confident" (p29). From the other side of a reunion, birth mother Debra Warila records, that when she met her son, "I had this feeling of completeness or wholeness, and that feeling has stayed" (Blau, 1993, p82). At the most fundamental level, a birth parent may recognise that reunion provides an opportunity for them to confirm their status as the progenitors of their child, an element of their identity that they perhaps had questioned in the aftermath of the adoption.

In his account of the experiences of birth fathers, Gary Clapton notes that, for those men who had been or were in contact with their child, the majority "experienced improved self-esteem" (2003, p174). One birth mother in Jones concludes that "I have more self-esteem because I searched ... I feel better about myself because I finally stopped holding in my grief and took action ... I *did* something to relieve my misery and declare my presence in the world" (1993, p199) [emphasis in the original].

Passmore and Coles found a general positive correlation between the well-being of birth fathers and their participation in reunion. They concluded: "It is perhaps not surprising that self-esteem was related to these reunion measures. However, caution is needed in interpreting cause and effect. For example, a successful reunion may help boost the self-esteem of birth fathers, but it is also possible that birth fathers who already have high self-esteem may approach reunions in a more positive light, which may in turn affect the way in which the reunion progresses. However, the positive effect of a successful reunion should not be under-estimated" (2008, p10). Passmore and Coles further noted: "The participants in the current study are not representative of birth fathers in general. In particular, the current study includes a higher proportion of birth fathers who have had reunions than reported in some previous studies (e.g., Clapton, 2003). About 70% of the birth fathers also currently had some contact with the birth mother" (2008, p12). They offered an explanation for the participation pattern: "Birth fathers who have 'come out of the closet' and have already told others about the relinquishment, may be more willing to speak about their experiences than others who have been more secretive and/or felt less supported. Birth fathers who have had successful reunions may also be at a more comfortable place in their lives where they are happy to talk about their experiences" (*ibid*).

For some people, mending deliberately involves all members of the family of origin *ie* the birth mother and the child, as well as the birth father. In their study of reunion, Gediman and Brown record "that several women achieved more complete senses of resolution when their sons and daughters met their birthfathers: feelings that unfinished business had been taken care of and that the circle, finally, was closed" (1991, p182). Sometimes members of the families of the respective birth parents, *eg* half-siblings, play a role. Birth mother Patricia Taylor records the benefits of working with the children of her marriage, the half-siblings of Kathi. "The recovery process has involved us all as we move to replenish self esteem (*sic*)" (1995, p294).

Increased self-esteem may in turn provide a useful lens through which to view the past in a more realistic light. An acknowledgment of loss and the processing of grief may allow the recovered person to view their past actions and reactions from a different, more honest perspective. For example, a birth mother may now accept that at the time of the adoption she was not stupid or negligent, but rather, naive. Instead of feeling inherently bad for allowing the adoption to take place, both birth parents may acknowledge that at the time, they were powerless; the life-changing decision was made <u>for</u>, not <u>by</u> them. This clarity may further enhance how they, today, feel about themselves, without in any way diminishing their recognition of the consequences of an adoption for all parties.

Speaking from the perspective of a birth mother, Sandra Falconer Pace (2004b) both laments the paucity of community awareness and summarises the path to recovery and its relationship to shame, grief and identity, when she writes:

> "As more of us who lost our children talk about our lifelong pain, it will be easier for all of us to set aside the bonds of shame. It will become easier to let go the trauma and anguish. It will take longer for our circle to set aside grief unresolved through all the years our children are lost to us, longer than those who don't experience it can understand. Our feelings have been disrespected and underestimated for decades. It may be that the enormity of the loss can never be resolved, only embraced as part of our identity. As we find our way to healing, as we let go of the pain and reclaim lives unshadowed by shame, we can welcome our children with joy and lighter hearts."

The Invisible Men of Adoption

Adoptive and birth parents

It is a fact that an adopted person has two sets of mothers and fathers. Post-reunion, it may be helpful for an adult adopted person to consider facilitating communication between his or her adoptive and birth parents. Taking the stance of the adoptive parent, Verrier observes "Many of the traits that you may have admired in your child can probably be found in some members of the birth family ... Get[ting] to know as many members of the birth family as possible ... will help you know and understand the ... personality of your child" (2003, p277).

Through meeting the adoptive parents, the individual birth parents may be able to fill in some of the information gaps for the period when the child was missing from their lives. Jim Shinn, a birth father, reports that he has "a really good relationship with [his son's] adoptive family," because "they are very open" (Blau, 1993, p125).

The view from support groups

In Melbourne, the Australian city in which I live, I have attended many support group meetings. I return, because, in this forum, I continue to learn about the legacy of adoption. After a decade of participation, I have reached some general conclusions that apply to the two main groups of attendees.

For birth mothers, overwhelmingly adoption represents loss, especially of their child. Other emotional responses radiate from this, their primary wound. Adopted persons often appear to be lost – to be disoriented and searching for their Self, a manifestation of the primal wound (the term used by Verrier, 1993 to describe the trauma suffered by the infant, as the result of being separated from his or her mother, soon after birth). I have noticed that many adopted persons have difficulty telling their story as a cohesive experience. Instead, they present a kaleidoscope of loose threads, which, it becomes apparent

The Invisible Men of Adoption

eventually, are interconnected. I have detected that whilst birth mothers often begin their (linear) narrative with the birth and departure of their child, adopted persons often labour to select a starting point, which perhaps is not surprising, given that they have no cognitive awareness of being separated from their birth parents. Bewilderment is less obvious amongst those adopted persons who have performed some recovery work, centred on their heritage and their identity.

For birth mothers and adopted persons alike, these observations from support groups confirm a direct correlation between, in the first instance, separation and wounding, and then later, as a result of dedicated effort, integration and healing.

CHAPTER 13

Love's labour's lost

"Sweet are the uses of adversity." — William Shakespeare

In discussions about the impact of adoption, there is another separation and reunion pairing that is frequently forgotten, or in some instances, deliberately ignored. It involves the two parents – the birth mother and the birth father. This oversight is at odds with the events that resulted in an adoption. An adult male and an adult female each contributed to the conception of the child. The mother carried the child through pregnancy, as a result of which she typically forged physical and emotional bonds with her unborn infant. An outcome of the in-utero bonding is that often the primary reunion sought is between the mother and her now adult child. Frequently, the reunion between father and child is secondary; given the fewer links a father has with his child, this hierarchy is to be expected.

Whilst I acknowledge that the quality of the original relationship between birth parents covers a broad spectrum, ranging from coercion to love, my emphasis here is on those relationships in which genuine, reciprocated affection was a feature. I accept, from listening to and reading the accounts of birth mothers that affectional relationships are not necessarily the norm. However, anecdotal evidence suggests that there are a considerable number of birth parents who retain positive thoughts for the other.

The birth mother and the birth father often separate (unless they later marry each other) at or about the time of the adoption.

The Invisible Men of Adoption

The reasons for this split are various. The mother may not have wanted the birth father to be involved. The birth father may have withdrawn his support. Social workers may have intervened and deliberately excluded the birth father from discussions about parenting. The two sets of parents may have made the decisions about the future of their children and their grandchild. As a consequence, the birth parents may feel that they relinquished control of their relationship to others; that this was against their wills and perhaps pushed them apart.

Some birth mothers and birth fathers may be envious of other couples who, faced with similar circumstances, kept their children. In these cases, the intervention of parents who sanctioned marriage (or in some cases insisted that the father and mother of the child get married) after the pregnancy became known, but before the child was born, resulted in a first child whose date of birth was less than nine months after the wedding. Whilst this situation often carried a stigma, particularly before the final quarter of the twentieth century, any disgrace tended to evaporate with time. Although the circumstances of the child's conception and birth may have created ructions within the extended families of both parents, nevertheless an adoption was avoided. Birth parents may be disappointed that they too did not have supportive families.

Affectional bonds exist within many relationships. When they are broken, they sometimes leave a residue of regret and missed opportunities. However, in situations where the couple create a child, and that child is lost to adoption, the presence (paradoxically, also the physical absence) of the third person, as evidence of intimacy between two adults, can be a potent reminder of the relationship that once existed between the birth mother and the birth father. Lovers who separate without having conceived a child lack the same reminder of the former affectional bond. Lovers who conceive a child and stay together see and appreciate the evidence of their intimacy every day.

Because an adoption sometimes coincides with the breaking of a meaningful adult relationship, it is reasonable to expect that the separated birth parents will experience post-adoption suffering.

Parting

The two adults of a severed relationship, the birth mother and the birth father, suffer losses. There is the loss of each to the other, as a physical parting. For some birth parents, the relationship may have been fleeting or perhaps the child was conceived as the result of rape. For others, there may be the loss of a serious relationship, often, according to studies by researchers such as Harkness (1991), Nicholls and Levy (1992), Carlini (1993), Clapton (2003) and Witney (2003), one that has spanned years. Clapton concludes, from his study of thirty birth fathers in the United Kingdom, that "For a considerable proportion of the men, the birth mother lived on in their feelings ..." (2003, p139). Stromberg found that when she interviewed a group of North American birth fathers, their "positive attitudes towards birth mothers" was a persistent theme (2002, p61), represented by "intense feelings and a remarkable amount of compassion" (p64). Writing from the other side of the severed relationship, Jones records that "a number of birthmothers hoped someday to resurrect and restore the loving relationship with the birthfathers that had perished under the traumas of relinquishment" (1993, pp234–235). However, notes Jones, not all dissolved relationships fall into this category; for some birth mothers the birth fathers "represented threatening, unsettling unfinished business" (p233).

Both birth parents may grieve their separation, particularly if their parting was in a situation that did not allow closure. The birth mother and birth father may not only have been excluded from the decision-making but also 'banned' from seeing each other again.

The grief experienced is liable to be disenfranchised. Residual feelings between birth parents are unlikely to be sanctioned by the community. Nor is the public likely to condone the open mourning of the loss of a relationship that might otherwise have culminated in marriage. In such circumstances the birth parents' grief may feel like a 'hole' in their lives. Jones is one author who acknowledges this form of "unresolved grief" (1993, p133).

Guilt may be an issue for both birth parents. A birth mother may feel that, in the face of parental disapproval, she failed to champion the man who wanted to marry her. She may consider that her lack of resolve not only damaged a loving relationship, but also, as a result, made it difficult for her to contemplate keeping her child. If the birth mother decides to act alone, she may feel guilty for excluding the birth father, of not providing him with the opportunity to participate in decisions about his child's future. A birth father who was unable to stand by the birth mother, either of his own volition or because of external pressures, may experience guilt for having let down the birth mother. In each case, it is the parent who feels they were unable to include the other who bears the brunt of the burden of guilt.

Whilst for a birth mother, father and child are discrete persons about whom often she can make separate decisions on the future of the respective relationships, a birth father's single decision necessarily embraces mother and child, for, by virtue of her pregnancy, the mother is carrying the child. Consequently, a birth father's reaction to loss is perhaps more likely to focus on mother and child as one. Because his relationship was with the woman and there is no father–child physical connection, during the pregnancy the man may find it difficult to look beyond the mother who is carrying the child. After the adoption, the birth father may realise that the child has a presence and that he has been responsible for breaking the bond between mother and child. This comprehension can perhaps further reinforce his guilt, particularly if the father has had the opportunity to see his infant after the birth and before the adoption. For the majority of birth fathers who do not see their new-born baby, their conscious connection with the actual events may remain centred on the person whom they knew and let down – the mother. This phenomenon perhaps explains why some birth fathers begin their interpersonal recovery work by seeking reconciliation with the mother of their child.

Jones notes that, even in circumstances where the birth parents married after the adoption, "many found that their marriages were haunted by the past ... the loss of their first child tended to make their happiness incomplete" (1993, p131). Jones continues, observing that "marriages between birthmothers and birthfathers were often speckled (*sic*) with scars and unhealed wounds from relinquishment" (p133).

A birth mother may be angry with the birth father because he has not stood by her. In other cases, the target of her anger could be her parents if they intervened and forbad the involvement of the birth father in decisions about the future of their child. Perhaps her anger is self-directed, if she believes that she failed to protect the birth father from the slings and arrows projected by her family and others.

A birth father may feel anger towards the parents, both his and the birth mother's, if they prevented him from supporting or having access to the birth mother. His anger might surface against himself for not assisting the birth mother. Some birth fathers express anger towards the birth mother, because they believe that she did not do enough to prevent their child from being adopted. Both birth parents may direct their anger against the constraints and the stigmatisation that society imposed upon them.

The impact of the loss of a child to adoption on subsequent intimate relationships is well documented in the literature. What has been overlooked is the effect the loss of a meaningful adult relationship has upon intimacy. If the plans for the birth mother and the birth father to marry were thwarted or reversed, it is no surprise that the outcomes might be a loss of faith in commitment and perhaps sincerity. In this situation, it is not only the loss of a child but a wariness about entering subsequent deep, long relationships that may occupy the minds of one or both birth parents and condition their approach to intimacy with others. Put another way, it may be the severing of the original adult relationship, not the adoption, which, for each birth parent has the greater influence on subsequent intimate relationships. If the original relationship between the birth parents was coercive, then the birth mother may be wary of intimacy with men. Here the quality of one uncaring relationship may again condition her attitude to future intimate relationships.

According to Jones, "Some [birthmothers] felt so deeply tied to the birthfathers that, even if they were no longer in contact, they could not allow any other men, even their own husbands, to come close" (1993, p110). By contrast, Clapton notes that in the circumstance where birth parents subsequently married each other, "All of the men talked of relationship difficulties arising from either an inability to discuss the adoption experience or their personal distress" (2003, p140). In this instance, the loss of their child has created communication issues within the marriage.

The fear of a rebuff, resulting from the circumstances of the original separation or a consideration of present relationships (*eg* does the spouse of their former sexual partner know about the child?), may interfere with one birth parent approaching the other to resolve outstanding issues surrounding their separation and the adoption.

Some birth parents feel compelled to compensate for the disempowerment they experienced when the adoption took place and they, as a man and a woman savouring a significant relationship, were separated. This may manifest itself in a need to exert control over subsequent relationships, to avoid the risk of being hurt by the actions of another person, in this case, their partner.

Depending on the circumstances that led to the pregnancy and the degree of involvement by the father in the decisions that led to the adoption, there may be a loss of trust, or at the very least, profound disappointment, experienced by the birth mother.

Most fundamentally, the parting of the birth parents can have a profound impact on their perceptions of themselves as mothers, fathers, lovers and worthy persons, core elements of their identity as individual human beings.

The Invisible Men of Adoption

A lingering residual affection between the birth parents may heighten the common responses to separation and loss. The spectre of 'what might have been' can, unless managed by each birth parent, become both a magnet and an obstacle to healing, which the birth father and the birth mother may find insurmountable.

Frequently, however, the motives for reconnecting are related to the conception and the shared contribution the birth parents have made to their child's heritage. One of the birth mothers in Gediman and Brown concludes that "her revived interest in the birthfather was connected to the bond they shared by virtue of having created this child" (1991, p180).

Reconciliation

Seldom are the results of the reunion between birth parents recorded. I have described my reunion with Kay, the birth mother of our son (Coles, 2004). A little has been written from the perspective of the birth mother.

Jones (1993) observes that many birth mothers found birth fathers who had experienced a "familiar array of guilty feelings and anxieties" (p242), including "incomplete grief, avoidance of intimacy, difficulties in parenting, generalized guilt and low self-esteem" (p241), feelings that resembled their own. She also refers to patterns of "loveless marriages, compulsions to be 'perfect', and children born in quick succession" (p242). Continuing, Jones records the experience of a particular birth father, from the perspective of the birth mother. "He replaced our relinquished child right away by marrying the very next girl he met and starting a family immediately. His marriage was not based on love. Like me, he married to have another child ... He *says* it's all in the past, but he still calls me a few times each year. He can't ... let go of me or our son" (p242) [emphasis in the original].

This theme of concern for mother and child is echoed by one of the birth fathers in Gediman and Brown: "He's searching for his former girlfriend and his child now because he feels he abandoned them both. He wants to make amends" (1991, p167). Cicchini (1993) and Clapton (2003) have noted similar responses amongst the birth fathers in their studies.

In the sparse literature about the views of birth mothers on reunions with birth fathers, there is a frequently expressed reaction; one of heightened emotions surfacing, *viz*: "Several of the birthmothers we interviewed felt that dealing with the birthfather and/or their feelings about him, was the most difficult part of the post-reunion experience" (Gediman and Brown, 1991, p181) and "[for] those who remained emotionally involved with the birthfathers, [the] renewed contact with their former lovers was as wrenching as the reunions [with their child]" (Jones, 1993, p234). Specifically, "[often] the passions and intense emotions aroused by the renewed contact were downright frightening to birthparents who had survived for decades by remaining rigidly 'in control' of their lives and relationships. The prospects of taking emotional risks, making dramatic changes, or sacrificing 'normalcy' were, for many, far too threatening" (Jones, 1993, p236). Sometimes, the reactions are tinged with disappointment, *viz* "the emotional aftermath of relinquishment combined with the events of the intervening years had changed both birthparents so profoundly that, even when the desires were mutual, the chances that their relationship would succeed were minimal" (Jones, 1993, p235).

For those who have performed no or little personal recovery work, reunion represents the first unbidden opportunity for suppressed grief to surface, bringing with it a plethora of feelings. Even if individual birth parents have addressed how they feel about themselves and their role in the original separation and perhaps also achieved reunion with the child, there are likely to be additional matters, complicated in some cases by a suppressed love for their former sexual partner, which may erupt when the birth parents reunite.

Individual reunions have unique qualities and there is no reason to suppose that a reunion between birth parents, typically adults at the time of separation and now, should be identical to that experienced between a birth parent and their child. The fundamentals of the parent–child relationship change between the adoption and reunion, usually over a hiatus that spans at least two decades. The child who was an infant when adopted, approaches reunion as an adult. There are some reports of reunions between mother and child, both adults, in which the parties feel drawn to revert to the time when parent and baby were separated. This parent–child regression is not a factor in reunions between birth parents, for typically they parted as adults and they return as (hopefully more mature) adults. Reuniting birth parents may however experience a reactivation of former intense feelings, akin to youthful euphoria. However, what parent–child and parent–parent reunions do have in common is that the participants have the same core issues, centred on loss and grief, to address.

Some mothers have reported that reunion helped resolve the relationship with the birth father. Jones records that "Although the loss of their fantasies devastated some women, others found that the truth finally set them free" (1993, p236). Gediman and Brown note another advantage: "[birthmothers] needed to meet and talk with the birthfather to 'unclog' [their] own repressed memories" (1991, p181). I can envisage that the dialogue might profitably cover matters such as the personal, family and social circumstances at the time of conception and the adoption, as well as how each has addressed the subsequent emotional pain. Such conversations provide an opportunity for both birth parents to ask and to answer questions.

Patricia Taylor is a birth mother who, with the birth father, Michael, welcomes the opportunity to talk "alone ... for the first time ever about our child." She assesses the benefits: "... we answered questions for each other which were still unresolved regarding the death of our relationship and the loss of our child [twenty] years before. Michael shared with me, as I did with him, the rituals he had developed over the years to deal with the loss of his daughter" (1995, p287).

The Invisible Men of Adoption

As a birth father, I contend that it is never too late for birth parents to engage in a dialogue. I do acknowledge that this might not be appropriate in some circumstances, for example if the child was conceived as the result of rape, where the relationship between the birth parents is underpinned by the spectre of threatening behaviour, or if one party does not wish to participate. However, I believe this dialogue does serve a useful purpose in circumstances where both birth parents accept that it is important they resolve personal issues surrounding the loss of their child, and further, agree that the discussion is integral to individual emotional healing.

Robinson proposes that if birth parents offer each other "the opportunity to address their grief issues and perform their personal recovery work ... prior to reunion with the [adult adopted person], then that adult will have the benefit of being reunited with birth parents ... who are more able to support the adopted adult child" (2004, pp79–80). In my opinion, conciliation between the birth parents reduces the possibility of an adult adopted person finding a mother and a father who bear ill-will towards each other, a distancing that may sabotage the prospects of a productive reunion between birth parent and child. Because of the potential benefits that may accrue for all three members of the family of origin, I believe it is appropriate that the first contact be between the birth mother and the birth father.

Sandra Falconer Pace (2004a), in a review of *Ever After: Fathers and the Impact of Adoption,* refers to the gains that accrued for her and her son, because she made contact with the birth father. "I had carried resentment against him for the loss of our son for 27 years ... but in talking with him I realized that he also grieved for the loss of his only son. He recognized that he'd made mistakes, just as I had and also recognized ... These realizations allowed me to let go of the resentment I felt towards him. It made reunion with our son much easier, since it allowed me to speak well of him to our son." Pace's personal experience raises an important point. The birth father who appeared to be callous and uncaring during the pregnancy and/or adoption may, over time, come to regret not standing by the birth mother.

One of the birth mothers interviewed by Fessler (2006) illustrates this turnaround. In the words of Nancy III, "He [the birth father of her child] called me one time and said, "I can't begin to tell you how awful I feel that you went through all of that alone." I was just blown away." The man, who at twenty had appeared mean, even arrogant, was, concluded Nancy III, "probably a much better person than I knew" (p256).

Karen (personal communication, 2005) is another who noticed a change in the birth father, when, in her case, she contacted him 35 years after the adoption. The man who had treated her harshly before her son was born now acknowledged the pain she had experienced as the result of losing her son, asked many questions about the welfare of his adult child, with whom Karen had had contact, and was pleased to hear that he was a grandfather. For Karen the outcomes of the initial conversation were positive. She felt that she could view the father of her child in a different light; he had changed and for the better. She was relieved that the contact she had hesitated to make, because of his past behaviour, had soothed her apprehensions and brought a degree of closure for her.

In circumstances where a detailed exploration of the issues is not feasible, I recommend that birth parents consider the ritual of communicating to honour their child's birthday. Both may benefit from an annual conversation, however brief this may be. Mason reports that "Even after Randy and his son's birthmother, Kim, married other people, he and Kim continued to annually commemorate their son's birthday" (1995, p14). I cannot imagine an adopted person, whether or not presently in contact with their birth parents, being unmoved by the knowledge that the birth mother and the birth father jointly have remembered and celebrated their birthday.

For those birth mothers who feel they have nothing to admire about the birth father of their child, I suggest they consider that he may now be prepared to acknowledge the consequences of his actions. This softening of attitude may allow both birth parents, and ultimately the child, to achieve positive outcomes. Forgiveness and the benefit of the doubt can provide cleared paths to healing, if exercised. For the birth father who was absent when the child was placed for adoption, the consequences of him now owning his actions and saying 'sorry' should not be underestimated. At the very least, it is unhelpful to dismiss his atonement outright.

Furthermore, I recommend that birth fathers who left the relationship with the birth mother before or at the time of the adoption, not expecting to hear from her again, respond considerately to her outreach. Through his receptiveness, the birth father may assist her healing. Her initiative may also allow him to recall and to come to terms with his role in the events that culminated in the adoption of their child.

There are birth parents who do not need to re-establish contact with one another, because they are married. Jones observes that "Some birthparent couples communicated openly, sharing their feelings about relinquishment, and searched for their children together. Others, however, did not. Occasionally birthmothers searched independently, compelled to separate their needs to find their children from their husbands' needs to suppress or deny the past" (1993, p238). Jones then offers a salient conclusion: "Most whose husbands protested their searches said that the birthfathers had neither grieved for their surrendered children nor supported the [birthmothers] in their own grief" (*ibid*). This demonstrable support embraces reunion, as well. On the subject of husbands, this time referring to those who do not have an adoption experience of their own, Jones writes of their key role: "Birthmothers who are happily married usually attribute their happiness, at least in part, to their husbands' unreserved acceptance of their pasts and support of their efforts to cope with their feelings" (1993, p137).

Jones has an overall conclusion about interpersonal recovery, as it applies to the seventy-two birth mothers she studied, *viz*, "By renewing contact and tending to long-festering wounds, some birthparents were able to acknowledge each other's pain and help each other to heal. When this occurred, reunions between birthparents were, in their own way, just as important as those shared with their children" (1993, p243). With reference to the reunion between birth parents and based on personal experience, I agree, wholeheartedly.

I can see the benefits of the two birth parents, as mature adults, engaging in a dialogue, thus bringing life's experiences to their discussion about loss, grief and healing.

Thus far, I have addressed the separation and mending between parent and child and the two birth parents as distinct events. There is, I suggest, a final step, that of reconciling the complete family of origin. This is a process that involves mother, father and child. Inclusion can be a significant gesture for all three persons, because it has the capacity to close the interpersonal wounds caused by the adoption. This 'grand' reunion acknowledges the ties that bind the members of the birth family, the people who are joined by the Triple Bond. I am not aware of such a reunion being documented in detail, *ie* from the perspectives of the three participants. However, I do know of one example of involvement told from the viewpoint of the birth father, up to but not including a tripartite reunion. Roger Stallings is a married birth father who remains in open contact with the married birth mother of his son – "I kept up with her life and she kept up with mine" (2004, p13). He continues: "Neither of us kept any secrets from our families ... and we never once forgot his birthday" (*ibid*). When Stallings searches for and locates his adult son, "I immediately called Marianne [the birth mother] and told her ..." (2004, p14). Marianne and son Terry meet, then Stallings and Terry ("We have developed the most incredible relationship" (*ibid*)).

I know of another example of a search initiated by the birth parents acting together ("Her father and I have always been in contact"). The birth mother and the birth father had each corresponded with their daughter, but not yet achieved reunion (Steer, 2004). Taylor (1995) is one writer who acknowledges the three members of the family of origin getting together, but she does not provide details about the outcome.

I can envisage the benefits of a tripartite reconciliation, but only after the three dyads of mother and father, mother and child, and father and child have dealt with their specific separation and integration issues and now feel that they are ready to face the prospect of being, for the brief time they are together, the family that an adoption broke apart. Because this 'complete' family reunion (a triad) potentially could cause intense emotions surrounding 'what might have been' to arise, I recommend it only for participants whose personal and interpersonal healing (as dyads) is well advanced.

I maintain that significant benefits can result if the three members of the family of origin are involved in reunion. The willing participation of all provides opportunities to explore the circumstances that led to the adoption, to answer questions and to celebrate the passing of genetic characteristics from parent to child. These matters make vital contributions to identity settlement and personal healing. In my view, full reunion is not accomplished if only two of the members of the birth family are involved. The birth family comprises mother, father and child. All played some role in the events surrounding the adoption. Post-adoption, all have roles to play in the exploration and comprehension of the original separation, for all were wounded by the same episode. Individually and collectively, the birth mother, the adopted person and the birth father are the beneficiaries, if they acknowledge the Triple Bond and co-operate to heal their wounds, via the dyads of mother–child, father–child and mother–father. At a physical level, separation breaks the Triple Bond, whilst reunion presents an opportunity for these tripartite links to be repaired. More fundamentally, the birth parents and the adopted child are joined by the act of conception and by their consanguinity, as well as psychologically and emotionally. It is this inner world that presents the greatest challenge for members of the family of origin.

CHAPTER 14

The enlightened family

"There are two kinds of light – the glow that illuminates, and the glare that obscures." — James Thurber

Preliminaries

There are plenty of birth fathers, in fact about as many as there are birth mothers and adopted people. The only birth father joke that I know may, in part, explain why, despite their significant numbers, these men remain seldom seen:

"Question to a birth father: *How many birth fathers does it take to screw in a light bulb?*
Answer by the same birth father: *Light bulb! What light bulb? I didn't screw any damn light bulb! It's not my light bulb and I don't know anything about it."*

Now plainly, here is a birth father who is in the pits of denial. He is the perfect illustration of a person who needs to come to his senses.

Then there is this claim, made by some adopted persons: "The people who adopted me are my real (for this read 'only') parents." Here is another statement that is embedded in an evasion of the facts. The truth is that all adopted persons have two mothers and two fathers – the birth parents and the adoptive parents.

The Invisible Men of Adoption

I believe that it is nigh impossible for the above people to live authentic lives, if they continue to withhold critical personal data from themselves, as well as from the family members who are affected by their avoidance strategies. For example, a birth father who continues to deny that he has fathered a child is unlikely to respond warmly to an outreach by his adult son or daughter. However, if the same father has found the courage and taken the time to reassess the facts about his role in the adoption, he is better placed to welcome an approach by his child.

Living with denial is living a lie. By embracing denial, you are consigning yourself to a compromised, partial life. Fundamentally, **the worst deceptions are those that we practice on ourselves**.

Here is another basic fact. **You cannot alter the events that are the foundation of your adoption experience, but you can change the way you think and feel about them.** In the second part of this statement lies the key to personal growth.

As the allies of denial, misconceptions and outright lies abound in the post-adoption world. 'All birth fathers are bastards', 'you are lucky, you were the chosen child', and 'your birth mother gave you up willingly' are common examples. Stereotypes and generalisations create labels and false perceptions, which can be difficult to overturn. As with shunning denial, challenging these misrepresentations requires pluck. In each case, there is a risk that you might not appreciate what you expose, because it may make life seem to be more complicated than formerly. Frequently, however, the difficulties you encounter are tied to the previous regime of deceit or avoidance, not the revelation of the truth.

I believe that there are four rehabilitation phases that we must complete before we are equipped to live an authentic life. Many people with adoption experiences will already have accomplished some of the steps; others will not yet have begun their exploration or are stalled along the way.

The Invisible Men of Adoption

Acknowledging the impact

The first step necessarily involves an acceptance that, for all members of the birth family, an adoption causes emotional pain. For some people, this means confronting and rejecting the self-deception and suppression they have practised for years.

Preserving secrets and deceiving ourselves are energy-sapping activities. A wise business colleague called Sam once told me his 'golden rule' – "I always seek and speak the truth about what happened, because if I tell other versions of the event, I am likely to be exposed, if not now, then eventually. Besides, misrepresentation is a time-waster." Here is a person who reveres honesty and openness, a man who appreciates the benefits of expending productive energy. Another way of expressing Sam's axiom is that manipulating or suppressing the truth adds needlessly to the complexity of life.

I maintain that we people with adoption experiences can advance only if we follow Sam's example. There is no denying that adoption causes distress. There is no denying that coming to terms with this distress can relieve the pain we all feel. There is no denying that those who look outside themselves for the direction that will transform their lives are likely to be dissatisfied. *Ipso facto*, the capacity for change lies entirely within our selves.

Accepting personal responsibility

Step two of the continuum involves taking responsibility for your feelings, as well as any past actions that have contributed to your present situation. For those who have blamed others for their predicament, *eg* being adopted or losing their child or the way they feel about themselves and others, this phase can be daunting. Some people become stuck here. Those who choose to remain bitter about their adoption experience, by, for example being intent on compensation for advice given or actions taken on their

The Invisible Men of Adoption

behalf decades earlier, stifle their own recoveries. The key to mending is to accept responsibility for personal actions, past and present; devolving this to others cannot promote personal development. For me, Stephen Covey (1990 and 2004) made a difference, in, for example: "Between stimulus and response there is a space. In that space lies our freedom and power to choose our response. In those choices lie our growth and our happiness" (Covey, 2004). Behind this sanguine statement lie two principles: 'Proactive people choose their responses; reactive people allow themselves to be acted upon' and 'sound choices are based on personal values, such as generosity, respect and honesty'.

Two adoption focussed axioms, which illustrate the benefits of candour and a preparedness to be proactive, arise from this base:

- **No one who has an adoption experience emerges unscathed. It is the degree to which each person admits to and addresses the impact of adoption on their life that makes the difference.**
- **The key to understanding your adoption experience and incorporating it into your life is the acknowledgment of cause and effect – when people are separated through adoption, they suffer a loss and experience grief.**

Grief is the natural and expected consequence of a loss. For members of the birth family, the grief is not of the type that we associate with a death. Those involved in an adoption loss are typically still alive. Thus adoption grief remains open or unresolved, although, paradoxically, it is also closed, in the sense that the loss goes unacknowledged and unmourned by the community. This core conflict creates the complexities that make the resolution of adoption separation issues such a challenging undertaking. Those without adoption experiences often are unaware of these difficulties. They may consider that the grief is not legitimate – there has been no death; also, they counter, the family members are able to meet each other, as adults. An adoption insider knows that the grief is real.

Beyond the observed grief manifestations such as numbness, sorrow and anger, the loss of a child to adoption contributes to issues surrounding identity, particularly feelings of self-worth. To mend, the birth parent and the (adult) child must undertake a programme of reconciliation and repair. This journey is initiated by the critical decision to move from being acted upon to taking action. Without your commitment to be proactive, personal healing is compromised.

Seeking to understand

Steps one and two – Acknowledgment and Responsibility – what I call the Validation phases of the Integration process, are the essential base, upon which the next phase – Understanding – builds. To this point, the personal changes you have made have been of the heart. Now it is time to involve the head.

I believe that the best way to make progress is to take practical measures. These have the objective of helping you to fathom the meaning of your adoption experience, to challenge any false beliefs you may have about your upbringing, as well as the community-based stereotypes. It is helpful to try to find out why you feel the loss of the other members of your family of origin and to comprehend the background to your fears and your feelings, which may include anger and guilt. It is useful to explore the social environment at the time the adoption took place. This delving is for one purpose – to give your adoption experience a realistic setting. You may find that, as a result of this probing, many of your earlier perceptions about yourself and others prove to be false. Furthermore, by working on and understanding your adoption experience, you may unearth the capacity not only to realise your self-potential but also to communicate your insights, for the accrued benefit of others.

The Invisible Men of Adoption

There are many avenues of exploration available to you. Up till now, much of your soul-searching has been solo. Some people prefer to continue working on the comprehension of their experience, alone. Personally, I think it is helpful to broaden your perspective and counter the risk of becoming insular, by learning about the experiences of others, who are likely to share, at the very least, aspects of your situation.

For those who choose to share their story orally, it is important that you seek a non-judgmental setting for your revelations. Support groups are often a good starting point. I recommend, rather than joining a mixed support group, comprising birth parents, adopted persons and adoptive parents, that at first you associate with a smaller group, one which represents your particular affiliation. Here, as you begin your release, you are likely to feel more at ease with those who share your perspective, whether, for example, it be mothers who have lost children to adoption or adopted persons who have grown up away from their family of origin. When you feel that you are ready to explore further, you may consider joining a broader group to listen to the views from the other side of the separation divide. In this setting you are also well placed to offer your perspective, to assist their understanding of what it means to you to be parted from the members of your birth family. (For birth fathers, this ideal sequence may not be possible. There may be insufficient fathers to form a dedicated support group. An alternative for these men may be to form an on-line chat group, before moving on to join a local mixed support group.)

Telling your story can be therapeutic, but remember also that this setting is a great opportunity for empathy and learning. It is likely that you will feel validated, as you hear people describe feelings that you had thought you alone had experienced. Probably, you will be offered fresh points of view to consider. Some of these may be confronting.

I have two cautions about support groups. Firstly, those birth parents and adopted persons who habitually attend support groups and come to rely upon them purely to narrate their

The Invisible Men of Adoption

circumstances and seek comfort *ie* sympathy, may consign themselves to remaining stuck in this phase for months, even years. Ultimately, I believe, the effectiveness of a support group is measured by the degree to which a balance is achieved between a) the sharing and recognition of allied experiences, and b) acknowledging diversity and presenting the opportunity for the individual to explore his or her own adoption experience. This leads to my second point. Support groups are effective only when in the hands of a skilled facilitator, a person capable of helping people help themselves.

Many books have been written about and by people with adoption experiences. Birth mothers and adopted persons are well represented; birth fathers barely. Edinburgh-based Gary Clapton and I are the only two birth fathers to have published books about birth fathers.

Books can be a valuable resource. I estimate that I have read more than sixty about adoption. Unfortunately, many are unhelpful, some misleading. There are four that have left an indelible, by which I mean overwhelmingly positive, imprint. What these publications have in common is their insightfulness, *ie* they dig beneath personal narratives and explain why people with adoption experiences feel the way they do. The first, chronologically, is Nancy Verrier's *The Primal Wound*, which, with good reason, has sold more copies than any other book about the consequences of adoption separation for adopted persons. Evelyn Robinson's books, *Adoption and Loss: The Hidden Grief* and *Adoption and Recovery: Solving the mystery of reunion* and *Adoption Reunion: Ecstasy or Agony?* are penetrating and well written. She presents her findings clearly and succinctly. In my opinion, Evelyn Robinson's books get to the nub of why we feel the way we do about our adoption experiences. The question and answer sections in her second and third books are brilliant – the advice is forthright, practical and refreshingly helpful.

However, there are many learning styles. For some, the old adage of 'sorrow shared is halved', usually accomplished through talking and listening, works. Other people prefer to express themselves through art or music. Anecdotally, I have heard that sometimes these latter mediums unearth dark personal emotions, which, if left unresolved within the session, may cause an individual to feel vulnerable and perhaps not fully in control of their actions, after they leave the venue. As is the case for support groups, a suitably qualified facilitator should be on hand.

Of those people who have access to counselling services, many find them helpful. The best counsellors are those who guide you to find your own solutions and who are pleased for your sake to celebrate the discoveries you have made about yourself. Responsible counselling acknowledges your emotional pain, and points out that it will continue, while stressing that it can be managed, so that the effects are less debilitating.

There is evidence that sound general skills, supported by a broad understanding of post-adoption issues, make for the most effective counselling. Some organisations stress the importance of a personal adoption experience to enhance a counsellor's effectiveness, but there is a risk here that any unresolved adoption issues carried by the counsellor may intrude upon the collaboration with the client.

Healing and integration

Healing, the second of the Action steps and the fourth phase overall, results from the effective processing and application of the work undertaken in the Understanding phase. There are two aspects of healing, involving the self and outreach to another member of the family of origin.

The inclusion of the interpersonal aspect under Healing is not meant to signify that the other party to a reunion is responsible, wholly or in part, for your recovery. You are entirely responsible for mending yourself.

As a result of completing the previous phases of the Integration process, you are well placed to incorporate your actions and reactions, which now have a context, successfully into your life and so achieve a measure of equilibrium. However, progress may not be linear. You may find that you are interrupted by self-doubt and apparent setbacks. For example, as an adopted person, your birth mother may parry your initial attempt to contact her. However, because of your initiative, she is now aware of your interest in her. Previously, she might have believed that she did not deserve to be contacted by you. The overturning of a key self-belief may take some time for her to process and your considerateness in not pushing harder for a reunion may create the space for her to address the burden of her post-separation grief and ultimately to reconsider your outreach. A birth father may discover that his search for the daughter he lost to adoption is thwarted by the absence of his name from the original birth certificate. This hiccup could create the opportunity for him to contact the birth mother, not only to seek her approval for his name to be added legally and retrospectively to the document, but also to discuss matters that were left unresolved at the time the adoption of their daughter took place. A birth mother may find it embarrassing to answer the question, "How many children do you have?" Experimentation with a range of statements, until she is comfortable with the way that she expresses the truth, may assist the birth mother to acknowledge that the child she lost to adoption is a *bono fide* member of her family. As a further benefit, her honesty may increase the community's awareness of adoption issues. In each of these examples, when the initiators are faced with challenges, it is their self-awareness, generosity and a positive outlook that stands them in good stead.

It is unlikely that the timing of individual healing initiatives will be concurrent for all three members of the birth family. The person instigating contact may discover that the person with whom they seek reunion has not yet started personal work or, at best, made limited progress. If the invitation to meet and to know is rejected or deferred, then the initiator who has done personal work is better placed to understand why the other may not yet be ready to consider a reunion. Whether or not reunion occurs, no member of a birth family is ever likely to rue the decision they made to understand their own adoption experience. Furthermore, the very act of making contact may leave a positive legacy – the trigger for the other to contemplate their adoption experience and initiate personal healing.

CHAPTER 15

To command the boundless sea

"You cannot discover new oceans unless you have the courage to lose sight of the shore." – Anonymous

The following suggestions are a guide to assist those people with an adoption experience to live a rich and fulfilling life. They are based on my observations and those of others who have written and spoken about the events that shaped their post-adoption lives.

Be open, be honest

Secrets and denial are deceitful. If you embrace these barriers to truth, you consign yourself to a partial life, one beset by angst and distrust. Efforts devoted to withholding information about the past undermine one's capacity to live in the present and to anticipate a promising future. The energy devoted to self-deceit and suppression is negative, with the likely consequence of inertia. Likewise, bitterness about and blaming others for your adoption experience blocks personal progress.

There is a remedy for an unfulfilling existence – to disown the inhibitors and install in their place the growth generators of honesty, openness and generosity. Confronting the unpalatable may seem risky, but I can guarantee that when you do take action, you will feel unburdened, more positive in your outlook and more welcoming of and appreciated by others. Dealing with the past is absolutely a risk worth taking.

The Invisible Men of Adoption

In my opinion, admitting to the denial you have practised to protect yourself is the first necessary step to personal healing. In doing so you may expose the secret about your past, which you have deliberately withheld from others, not because of the content of your revelations, but rather what you believed they might think of you. Fundamentally, recovery is not possible for the person who is intent on preserving secrets, whether this be self-deceit and/or deliberately withholding information from others.

Anger, used productively, rather than with bitterness, to effect change, may assist self-enlightenment and provide guidance or inspiration for others. The application of positive energy and personal responsibility are essential, if you aim to live a rewarding life.

Share and assimilate

I believe that sharing your adoption experience not only with yourself but also with others is therapeutic. Support groups are often a good starting point, particularly for those who prefer oral and aural communication.

If, however, you find that your explorations are driven by a rage founded on blame and bitterness, I suggest that you seek professional help from an expert. Some psychologists and counsellors have little or no understanding of the contrasting closed (the repressed emotional pain often goes unrecognised) and open (not only are the separated members of the birth family still alive, but also they are likely to experience a delayed reaction to the initial loss when they reunite) aspects of the grief that accompanies adoption, so make sure that you ask some background questions before you choose and begin paying.

If you are a birth father, then there are additional factors for the helping professions to consider. Fathers were often excluded from the adoption process and in many instances their names are absent from the adoption records. The compounded guilt, manifesting itself as double jeopardy, which is experienced by some birth fathers, can complicate the men's reactions to the original separation of the birth family, their search patterns and personal and interpersonal healing.

Explore the background

Healing may benefit from a retrospective analysis of the circumstances that resulted in an adoption. In the case of birth parents, your family may not have been close-knit and therefore not in a position to offer you support upon hearing the news of unplanned motherhood or fatherhood. Community attitudes of the time perhaps conditioned the family to promote the adoption option and so protect themselves from stigmatisation. Those arranging the placement of the child may simply have reinforced plans already decreed by the extended family, albeit in many cases, without the specific say-so of the birth mother and/or the birth father.

The guilt and the shame that birth parents often heap upon themselves may, with the passing of time and an increasing awareness of the circumstances in which the adoption took place, become less burdensome. Dialogue between the birth parents and their respective parents may enhance a comprehension of the environment in which each birth parent was raised and the conditions that precipitated their being separated from their child. These discussions may unblock the past.

For adopted persons, who have no cognitive awareness of the events surrounding their adoption, the available avenues may be reading about and listening to the experiences of others. Social histories can assist; also the narratives of other adopted persons who have achieved reunion. The circumstances of their own adoption, told frankly by the birth parents, may, if reunion occurs, be the best source of information.

The Invisible Men of Adoption

Be self-responsible

Ideally, personal healing should be undertaken before interpersonal healing. After completing the inside work, the individual is better prepared for the reunion, the main purpose of which is to address the effects of an adoption on the relationships between the birth family members.

Sadly, many people enter reunion without adequate preparation. Some believe, falsely, that reunion will resolve their adoption issues and how they feel about themselves. These people perhaps do not understand the meaning of their adoption experience, but expect to be mended by meeting a family member from whom they were separated. This devolution of responsibility not only places unwarranted pressure on the other person, but it also creates a self-expectation that is unlikely to be met.

If, however, you have prepared well and also are fortunate enough to enter reunion with another member of your birth family who has also worked on their adoption issues, then the possibilities for a sustained and fulfilling relationship, are, I believe, enhanced. Do not wait for reunion to begin work on understanding what adoption means for you. If you have not already started, now is the time.

Use technology wisely

In reunion, it is important to proceed at the pace of the slower person. Today, where social networking sites such as Facebook are used by many, this objective may be threatened. Among some searchers, Facebook and its ilk have fostered the expectation of instant gratification, which they equate with the ease of access to information. In this situation, expectations of an immediately forged relationship are likely to be dashed.

The potential recipients of outreach may unthinkingly place identifying information on social network sites when they are not yet ready for reunion. These persons can experience distress when they are approached. The reunion sought by the person initiating the outreach may founder on the damage caused to the recipient.

There is another complication. Given that Facebook serves as an electronic noticeboard, privacy can be compromised, as is the capability to limit the audience, unless properly managed. Whilst Facebook is a helpful tool when used to search for a person, it is unwise to use it for initiating communication with a view to forging a lasting reunion.

To summarise – those contemplating reunion are best served by reminding themselves that consideration for the other is foremost.

Don't neglect the birth father

Sadly, the concerns of birth fathers have been overlooked in the past. The bias by some social workers and family members against birth fathers has contributed to this marginalisation. As a consequence, birth fathers have remained misunderstood and typically in the background. The responsibility to rectify this situation sits primarily with birth fathers.

For adopted persons and birth mothers, as well as professional persons such as counsellors and social workers, I suggest that acknowledgment and tolerance be accorded birth fathers. It may prove useful to contemplate the possibility that the father has, with the passage of time and maturity, become remorseful and troubled about his part in those long ago events.

The helping professions can help themselves and their clients by becoming informed about the impact of adoption on all participants, including birth fathers. The inclusion of birth fathers in adoption policy formulation and welcoming them to support groups are further concrete demonstrations of their recognition by other members of the Adoption Sandwich.

The Invisible Men of Adoption

Honour the initiative taken by the other party

If you are the recipient of an outreach, pause and contemplate the broader context of what this approach means. Of course, your reaction is important, but beyond the personal, it is worthwhile contemplating what the initiator has to offer you. It is a fact that the overwhelming majority of those who initiate outreach do so with the purest of intentions, *ie* to seek reunion with family members. By initiating a search, birth parents make it clear that they love and want to know their adult children. Through their action, adopted persons who reach out to their birth mother and/or birth father convey a similar message.

Family of origin members know, albeit with varying degrees of self-acknowledgment, that it is possible they will be approached and asked to participate in reunion. It is disheartening, given this background, to hear that some recipients of requests for contact and reunion see the invitation as threatening and intrusive. Some say that they don't have time to fit the requester into their lives. In the eyes of the searcher, this response, even if a throwaway comment, seems dismissive and to diminish the family of origin. Other recipients of outreach do not reply; they choose to remain silent. That he or she as the initiator has taken a risk, given that they are ignorant of what stage of processing your adoption experience you have reached, is a factor worth considering by the recipient. As a reciprocal gesture, rather than parrying the contact, you might best become a risk-taker yourself, and in replying in a positive manner, create the opportunity to participate in a voyage of mutual self-discovery.

However, if you admit in your response that you wish to have time to prepare yourself better for the reunion, this is a positive sign that you wish to engage, but at an unspecified time in the future. At a base level, if you are unable to make a commitment, a simple acknowledgement is better than nothing at all.

It is important to recognise the truth about key relationships. The birth mother, the birth father and the adult adopted person, who is their son or daughter, are members of the family of origin. Because of their consanguinity and the circumstances of conception, the three individuals can never become merely casual acquaintances or friends, as claimed by some who have reunited; they are and always will be family.

Stay positive in the face of setbacks

If you reach out, seeking reunion with the person from whom you were separated at the time of the adoption and you receive a rebuff, try not to take it personally. It is likely that the person whom you have contacted has not rejected you. Rather it is probable that they have not yet faced their adoption issues, so as to be in a position where they feel ready to join you in reunion. Regrettably, some recipients of outreach find it difficult to admit that adoption has had an impact upon their lives; others recognise that adoption has affected them, but are unwilling (yet) to grant this concession.

If you are the initiator, the rebuff may seem harsh and permanent, but I suggest that you do not try to guess the reasons why your offer has been declined. You might consider how it was for you at the time when you felt uncomfortable, perhaps even petrified about facing your adoption issues. Strive to be patient and exercise consideration. You can draw solace from the fact that the other member of your family of origin is aware that you care about them.

Approaching a parent–child reunion from the perspective of what you can offer, rather than what you want is beneficial for both parties. For a birth parent, presenting opportunities for the other to know you, to be available to answer questions about the circumstances of the adoption and any other matters, such as heritage and well-being, displays humanity.

I believe that it is not threatening if you occasionally remind the person with whom you seek reunion that you continue to care about them. A birthday and Christmas can be the appropriate times to send your best wishes. I suggest that you keep your written messages short, simple and unemotional. Because you send a card does not mean that you should anticipate one in return, either thanking you, or for your birthday or at Christmas time. A useful way to consider your reaching out twice a year is to view it as an opportunity to issue the other person with a subtle invitation to participate in reunion. You are, without saying as much, keeping the possibility of a reunion open, by conveying your wishes in a caring, non-threatening manner. I believe that there would be few recipients who would object to the spirit of the messages. Another possible benefit for the recipient is that they may feel reassured that you, the sender, were not offended by their decline of your original offer. Further, through his 'no-obligation' approach, the initiator of the regular communication appears to be prepared to give you, the recipient, space and wait until **you** are ready for reunion. My son admitted that my sending him birthday cards for a decade was a positive factor in his decision to meet me.

Bear in mind, however, that nobody is immortal. In the situation where the recipient of the cards is the adopted person, birth parents, like everybody else, have a finite life and they may have expired of old age (and worn out their patience!) before their 'child' is ready to sanction reunion.

A message for birth fathers

I encourage more birth fathers to own up to their adoption experiences. Considering what I have learned about myself and what I have heard from a regrettably small sample of birth fathers, I maintain that admitting to and addressing the past is therapeutic.

As with other members of the separated family, to progress a birth father must be adventurous and prepared to reach out. For him, this involves contacting and seeking reunion with the adult adopted person, as well as the birth mother. A birth father must be prepared to give of himself to assist their mending – the birth mother and the adult adopted person can choose whether or not to avail themselves of the opportunity that he offers. A birth father's willingness to be available applies not only to his taking the initiative, but also sets the tone and defines the content of his response to an outreach made by his adult child or the birth mother.

Anecdotally, it seems that many birth fathers remain timid, afraid of the consequences of communicating with the other members of the family of origin. My view is that it is better to try and to know, than not to have tried at all.

I concede that there are birth fathers who are not aware that they have fathered a child who was subsequently adopted. Also, I recognise that some jurisdictions have in the past disallowed or discouraged the entry of the birth father's name on the birth record. In situations where the birth father knows his status, he may, legally, be in a position to correct this oversight. However, it seems that few men choose to acknowledge their paternity retrospectively. When Passmore and Coles conducted their study in 2008, they found that many of the birth fathers canvassed were unaware that they could arrange to have their name included on the original birth certificate, many years after the birth of their child.

Unfortunately, there are some birth fathers who believe, because their name is absent from the original birth certificate, that they are not entitled to know their child.

These matters may explain, in the case of New Zealand (where such statistics are available), the discrepancy between applications made by birth mothers and birth fathers for identifying information about their adopted children.

Sadly, also, birth fathers are present in small numbers at public forums about post-adoption matters and, I suspect, as initiators of reunion. Only birth fathers can alter this imbalance. I urge them to do so, otherwise the voice of the birth father will remain subdued and the stereotype of the callous, invisible man preserved, to the detriment of all affected by adoption. Birth fathers have much to offer to themselves, the other members of the family of origin and the community.

Be inclusive, be generous

During the grieving and the healing phases, I believe that all members of the family of origin warrant consideration. An adoption coincided with the disintegration of a family; these same three family members display awareness and responsibility if they ensure that they integrate their adoption experiences into their lives. Each also has the opportunity to demonstrate generosity, by assisting the other family members with their recoveries. Mother, father and adult child all benefit if they each display a willingness to be equal participants in interpersonal recovery work. The three dyads of mother and child, father and child and the two parents were separated by the adoption. To promote personal integration, I recommend that the same pairings seek reunion, from which interpersonal reconciliations may result. If the complete triad of birth mother, birth father and adopted person do not involve themselves in search and reunion, then, in my view, personal and interpersonal healing for each is, by definition, compromised.

Recover your self and live

I maintain that people with adoption experiences cannot move forward until they have dealt with the barriers and the inhibitors associated with the past.

For healing to occur, however, personal foundations have to be laid. The will to advance and a willingness to be transparent with yourself and others are essential elements. A commitment to task completion and tenacity are mandatory qualities. These few basics are the precursors to action.

Persons with adoption experiences cannot, I believe, consider themselves whole unless and until they have acknowledged their losses, processed the accompanying grief and incorporated the effects of the original parent–child separation into their lives. (For birth parents, there is also the severance of their relationship to consider.) Grieving the loss caused by an adoption is healthy and productive. To address the grief displays awareness, personal responsibility and commitments to openness, honesty and growth. Your generosity embraces the people you care about, including yourself – a potent, positive legacy for all directly affected by the original adoption. Letting go of any blame or resentment and forgiving yourself and others encompassed by your adoption narrative confirms your generosity. For those who are not ready to reconsider their position, I urge patience. Given time, they may be influenced by your generosity.

Ignoring the loss, grief and other consequences may have a negative, aggravating effect, which is likely to curb personal growth. In my view, pretending that the adoption has had no impact on your life is not a feasible alternative, unless you wish to condemn yourself to a constrained existence. To accept this latter scenario mutely is to waste the opportunity for a life celebrated.

Figure 4 summarises the personal management of the impact of adoption. Participants have a clear choice between letting the growth inhibitors of deceit, secrecy and denial hold sway or embracing the growth generators of honesty, openness and generosity. The diagram displays the consequences of being beholden to restraining self-beliefs. More importantly, it highlights the personal benefits of opting to be proactive; of creating and being in command of your new paradigm.

"The end of separation is meeting again." – Turkish proverb

Figure 4: Post-adoption Pain and Healing – A Summary

Anxieties (based on self-beliefs) + Growth Inhibitors	...	Commitments (driven by self-determination) + Growth Generators

Guilt – caused adoption to occur
 	
Shame – deserve misfortune   *Deceit*
 	
Disempowerment – emotional turmoil occurs when not in control of own destiny
                                               Secrecy
 	
Rejection – come to expect, because of personal deficiencies
 	
Intimacy – getting close may re-enact original loss   *Denial*
		Acknowledge the impact of the adoption on you
		                                          Honesty
		
		Take personal responsibility for addressing the pain
		
		Explore and understand your reactions to loss and grief *Openness*
		
		Mend, both by delving in and reaching out
		
		                                        Generosity

⇓ ⇓		⇓ ⇓
Consequences - Self-protection - Interpersonal inertia - Stuck in the past - Fragmented, static existence		**Results** - Self-discovery (personal recovery and well-being) - Interpersonal recovery (reunion) - Live in the present; welcome the future - Integrated, fulfilling life

References

"The outward wound and the inward healing." — Les Misérables, *by* Victor Hugo

Andersen, Robert S. *Why Adoptees Search: Motives and More*, 'Child Welfare', Volume 67, Number 1, pp 16–19, 1988

Andersen, Robert S. *The Nature of Adoptee Search: Adventure, Cure or Growth*, 'Child Welfare', Volume 68 Number 6, pp 623–632, 1989

Anderson, Carole J. *Why Won't My Birthmother Meet Me?* Concerned United Birthparents, Inc, USA, 1982

Anderson, Carole J. *Thoughts to Consider for Newly Searching Adoptees*, Concerned United Birthparents, Inc, USA, 1997

Biddulph, Steve. *Manhood: a book about setting men free*, Finch Publishing, Australia, 1994

Blau, Eric. *Stories of Adoption: Loss and Reunion*, NewSage Press, USA, 1993

Bouchier, Patricia, Lambert, Lydia and Triseliotis, John. *Parting with a Child for Adoption: The Mother's Perspective*, BAAF, United Kingdom, 1991

Bradley, Seamus. *The shell shock of discovery*, 'The Age', Melbourne, Australia, 21 January 2001

Brodzinsky, David M, Schechter, Marshall D and Henig, Robin Marantz. *Being Adopted: The Lifelong Search for Self*, Random House, USA, 1993

Brosnan, Thomas. Keynote Address to the 1996 National Maternity and Adoption Conference, 'issues', Number 3, Feb–March 1997, pp10–12

Brown, Rob. *Father's Day*, 'ARCS Quarterly Newsletter', Spring 2002, pp7–9

The Invisible Men of Adoption

Bryson, Bill. *A Short History of Nearly Everything*, Doubleday, UK, 2003

Butler-Bowdon, Tom. *50 Self-Help Classics*, Simon & Schuster (Australia) Pty Limited, Australia, 2001 [Quoted passages are from the summary of *An Intimate History of Humanity* by Theodore Zeldin]

Carlini, Heather. *Adoptee Trauma: A Counselling Guide For Adoptees*, Morning Side Publishing, Canada, 1993

Cicchini, Mercurio. *Development of Responsibility: The Experience of Birth Fathers in Adoption*, Adoption Research & Counselling Service Inc, Australia, 1993

Clapton, Gary. *Birth fathers' secret pain*, 'The Age', Melbourne, Australia, 19 August 2000

Clapton, Gary. *Perceptions of Fatherhood: Birth fathers and their Adoption Experiences*, 'NORCAP News', Number 59, Spring 2001, pp4–5

Clapton, Gary. *Birth Fathers and their Adoption Experiences*, Jessica Kingsley Publishers, United Kingdom, 2003

Coles, Gary. *Being a Birthfather*, 'Proceedings of "Adoption Looking Forward Looking Back" Conference', Canterbury Adoption Awareness and Education Trust, New Zealand, 1998, pp119–120

Coles, Gary. *To Search or not to Search: that is the question*, 'VOICE', Summer Edition, January 2002

Coles, Gary. *Ever After: Fathers and the Impact of Adoption*, Clova Publications, Australia, 2004

Coles, Gary. *Transparent: Seeing Through the Legacy of Adoption*, Mermerus Books, Australia, 2005

Collins, Pauline. *Letter to Louise*, Bantam Press, United Kingdom, 1992

Covey, Stephen R. *The Seven Habits of Highly Effective People*, The Business Library, Australia, 1990

Covey, Stephen R. *The 8th Habit: From Effectivenes to Greatness*, Simon & Schuster, United Kingdom, 2004

Dent, Mark. *A good day to walk: My encounter with bone cancer*, David Lovell Publishing, Australia, 1997

Deykin, Eva Y, Patti, Patricia and Ryan, Jon. *Fathers of adopted children: A study of the impact of child surrender on birthfathers*, 'American Journal of Orthopsychiatry' Volume 58, 1988, pp240–248

Doka, Kenneth. *Disenfranchised Grief: Recognising Hidden Sorrow*, Lexington Books, USA, 1989

Fessler Ann. *The Girls Who Went Away*, Penguin Books, USA, 2006

Fisher, Florence. *The Search for Anna Fisher*, Michael Dempsey, United Kingdom, 1973

Fredman, Neil. *Why this adoptee doesn't want to find his birth mother*, 'The Age', Melbourne, Australia, 19 November 2001

Gediman, Judith and Brown, Linda. *BirthBond: Reunions Between Birthparents and Adoptees – What Happens After...*, New Horizon Press, USA, 1991

Gibran, Kahlil. *The Prophet*, William Heinemann Ltd, United Kingdom, 1926

Griffith, Keith C. *The Right To Know Who You Are: Reform of Adoption Law with Honesty, Openness and Integrity*, Katherine W Kimbell, Canada, 1991

Griffith, Keith C. *Key Issues in New Zealand Adoption*, 'Proceedings of "Adoption Looking Forward Looking Back" Conference', Canterbury Adoption Awareness and Education Trust, New Zealand, 1998, pp21–27

Harkness, Libby. *Looking for Lisa*, Random House, Australia, 1991

Hart, Jane. *My Birth Father's Legitimate Grief*, 'Decree', American Adoption Congress, Spring/Summer 2000

Hartman, Ann. *Secrecy in Adoption*, in Evan Imber-Black, *Secrets in Families and Family Therapy*, WW Norton & Company, USA, 1993, pp86–105

Hochman, Gloria, Huston, Anna and Prowler, Mady. *Issues facing Adult Adoptees*, 'issues', Number 12, Oct–Dec 1998, pp11–12

Holm, Rod. *The Adopted and Difficult Adolescent*, 'Proceedings of 7th Australian Adoption Conference', Hobart, 2000, pp329–339

The Invisible Men of Adoption

Howard, Sally. *Finding me in a paper bag: Searching for both sides now*, Gateway Press, Inc, USA, 2003

Howarth, Ann. *Reunion*, Penguin Books, New Zealand, 1988

Howe, David and Feast, Julia. *Adoption, Search and Reunion: The long term experience of adopted adults*, The Children's Society, United Kingdom, 2000

Imber-Black, Evan. *An Overview*, in Evan Imber-Black, *Secrets in Families and Family Therapy*, WW Norton & Company, USA, 1993, pp18–27

Inglis, Kate. *Living Mistakes: Mothers who consented to adoption*, Allen & Unwin, Australia, 1984

Jones, Mary Bloch. *Birthmothers: Women who have relinquished babies for adoption tell their stories*, Chicago Review Press, USA, 1993

Kaplan, Sharon and Silverstein, Deborah. *Seven Core Issues in Adoption*, in Keith Griffith, *The Right To Know Who You Are: Reform of Adoption Law with Honesty, Openness and Integrity*, Katherine W Kimbell, Canada, 1991, Section 2, pp1–4

Lifton, Betty Jean. *Lost and Found: The Adoption Experience*, Harper & Row, USA, 1988 [NB: First published by Dial Press in 1979]

Lifton, Betty Jean. *Journey of the Adopted Self: A Quest for Wholeness*, Basic Books, USA, 1994

Lifton, Betty Jean. *The Adoptee's Journey*, 'Journal of Social Distress and the Homeless', Vol 11, No.2, April 2002, pp207–213

Lowe, Heather. *What you should know if you're considering adoption for your baby*, Concerned United Birthparents, Inc, USA, undated

MacKay, Linda. *Creating a separate identity: differentiation and the experience of adoption*, 'issues', Number 32, Dec 2004–Feb 2005, pp12–19

McCann, Rex. *On Their Own: Boys growing up underfathered*, Finch Publishing, Australia, 2000

Marshall, Audrey and McDonald, Margaret. *The Many-Sided Triangle: Adoption in Australia*, Melbourne University Press, Australia, 2001

Marshall, Dianne. *Would you Recognise the Loss and Grief of Adoption?*, 'issues', Number 14, April–July 1999, pp1–8

Mason, Marilyn J. *Shame: Reservoir for Family* Secrets, in Evan Imber-Black, *Secrets in Families and Family Therapy*, WW Norton & Company, USA, 1993, pp29–43

Mason, Mary Martin. *Out of the Shadows: Birthfathers' Stories*, O J Howard Publishing, USA, 1995

Mason, Mary Martin. *The Missing Link in Adoption: Birthfathers*, 'CUB Communicator', April/May 1997

Murray, Mary. *My Journey of Reunion: A Work in Progress*, 'ARMS Victoria Newsletter', Autumn 2002

Nankervis, Julie. *Redrawing the Triangle: The Role of Natural Fathers in Infant Adoption post 1984 (Vic) Adoption Act*, Presented to the Victorian Standing Committee on Adoption & Alternative Families, Australia, June 1991

Newbould, Jennifer. *ARCS News*, 'ARCS Quarterly Newsletter', Winter 2003, p2

New South Wales Legislative Council. *Releasing the Past; Adoption Practices 1950–1998: Final Report*, Parliamentary Paper Number 600, NSW Standing Committee on Social Issues, Australia, 2000

Nicholls, Rosemary and Levy, Mina. *Relinquishment Counselling of Birth Fathers*, Chapter 6 of *The Search for Self*, ed Phillip and Shurlee Swain, The Federation Press, Australia, 1992

NSW Committee on Adoption, Inc. *Down the Track: Outcomes of Adoption Reunions*, Australia, 1990

NSW Committee on Adoption and Permanent Care, Inc. *Further Down the Track: A Collection of Personal Experiences of Adoption Reunions,* Australia, 2001

O'Shaughnessy, Tim. *Adoption, Social Work and Social Theory*, Avebury, United Kingdom, 1994

Pace, Sandra Falconer. *Review of "Ever After: Fathers and the Impact of Adoption"* on the website of the 'Canadian Council of Natural Mothers', 2004a

The Invisible Men of Adoption

Pace, Sandra Falconer. *Shame*, on the website of the 'Canadian Council of Natural Mothers', 2004b

Pace, Sandra Falconer. *Things Have Changed: What Has Changed in Adoption Practice and What Remains the Same*, on the website of the 'Canadian Council of Natural Mothers', 2005

PARC. *'Client Stories: Kevin's Story*, 'Branching Out': Newsletter of the Post Adoption Resource Centre, Vol. 5, No. 3, 1998, pp19–21

PARC. 'Branching Out', Volume 11, Number 3, October 2004

Passmore, Nola and Coles, Gary. *The Impact of Relinquishment on Birth Fathers*, Paper presented at the Ninth Australian Adoption Conference, Sydney, 2008

Passmore, Nola and Coles, Gary. *Birth Fathers' Perspectives on Reunions with their Relinquished Children*, Paper presented at the 9th Annual Conference of the APS Psychology of Relationships Interest Group, Brisbane, 2009

Passmore, Nola, Feeney Judy and Foulstone, Alex. *Secrecy within adoptive families and its impact on adult adoptees*, 'Family Relationships Quarterly', Number 5, 2007

Phillips, Zara. *Chasing Away the Shadows: An Adoptee's Journey to Motherhood*, Gateway Press, USA, 2004

Portuesi, Donna. *Silent Voices heard: Impact of the Birth Mother Experience Then and Now*, 'Decree', American Adoption Congress, Spring/Summer 2000, pp5–7

Robinson, Evelyn. *Grief associated with the loss of children to adoption*, 'Proceedings of The Sixth Australian Conference on Adoption', Brisbane, 1997, pp268–293

Robinson, Evelyn. *Adoption and Loss: The Hidden Grief*, Clova Publications, Australia, 2000a

Robinson, Evelyn. *Some thoughts on anger*, 'ARMS South Australia Newsletter', Autumn Edition, April 2000b, pp10–11

Robinson, Evelyn. *Adoption and Loss: The Hidden Grief*, unpublished presentation to ARCS, Perth, Western Australia, 2001a

Robinson, Evelyn. *Adoption and Loss: The Hidden Grief*, unpublished presentation to BirthLink, Edinburgh, Scotland, 2001b

Robinson, Evelyn. *Post-adoption grief counselling*, 'Adoption & Fostering', Volume 26 Number 2, 2002, pp57–63

Robinson, Evelyn. *Adoption and Loss: The Hidden Grief [Revised Edition]*, Clova Publications, Australia, 2003

Robinson, Evelyn. *Adoption and Recovery: Solving the mystery of reunion*, Clova Publications, Australia, 2004

Robinson, Evelyn. *Adoption Reunion: Ecstacy or Agony?*, Clova Publications, Australia, 2009

Roche, Heather. *A Journey not Travelled: A qualitative study seeking to understand the experience of mature age adult adoptees who have chosen not to search for their biological families*, VAFT News, Vol. 31, No. 3, June 1999, pp7–16

Russell, Marlou. *Adoption Wisdom: A Guide to the Issues and Feelings of Adoption*, Broken Branch Productions, USA, 1996

Sachdev, Paul. *Adoption reunion and after: a study of the search process and experience of adoptees*, 'Child Welfare', 71, 1992, pp53–68

Saffian, Sarah. *Ithaka*, Dell Publishing, USA, 1998

Schaefer, Carol. *The Other Mother: a woman's love for the child she gave up for adoption*, Soho Press, Inc, USA, 1991

Schooler, Jayne. *Searching for a Past: The Adopted Adult's Unique Process of Finding Identity*, Pinon Press, USA, 1995

Seitz, Karyn. *Journey Through Adoption*, Australia, 2000 [self-published]

Severson, Randolph. *Dear birthfather,*, House of Tomorrow Productions, USA, undated

Shawyer, Joss. *Death by Adoption*, Cicada Press, New Zealand, 1979

Silverman, Phyllis R. *Helping Women Cope with Grief*, Sage Publications, USA, 1981

Silverman, Phyllis R, Campbell, Lee, Patti, Patricia and Style, Carolyn Briggs. *Reunions between Adoptees and Birth Parents: The Birth

Parents' Experience, 'Social Work', November–December 1988, pp523–528

Small, Joanne. *Working with Adoptive Families*, 'Public Welfare', Summer, 1987, pp33–41

Sorosky, Arthur D, Baran, Annette and Pannor, Reuben. *The Adoption Triangle*, Corona Publishing Co., USA, 1989 [NB: Originally published by Anchor Press/Doubleday in 1978]

Stallings, Roger. *Birthfathers and Miracles*, 'issues', Number 31, Sept–Nov 2004, pp13–14

Steer, Isabella. *Melissa*, Newsletter of the Association of Relinquishing Mothers (Vic) Inc., Spring 2004

Stiffler, LaVonne Harper. *Synchronicity and Reunion: The Genetic Connection of Adoptees and Birthparents*, FEA Publishing, USA, 1992

Stromberg, Michelle Denise. *Birth fathers and the Adoption Experience: A Narrative Exploration of the Birth Father Perspective on Adoption*, A Thesis Submitted to the Faculty of Graduate Studies and Research in Partial Fulfillment of the Requirements for the Degree of Master of Social Work, University of Regina, Canada, 2002

Taylor, Patricia E. *Shadow Train*, Gateway Press, Inc, USA, 1995

Tracy, Brian. *Maximum Achievement: Strategies and Skills That Will Unlock Your Hidden Powers to Succeed*, Fireside, USA, 1995

Tugendhat, Julia. *The Adoption Triangle*, Bloomsbury, United Kingdom, 1992

VANISH. *The VANISH Resource Book*, VANISH Publications, Australia, 1998

VANISH Incorporated. 'VOICE', Winter Edition, May 2004

Van Keppel, Margaret, Midford, Suzanne and Cicchini, Mercurio. *The Experience of Loss in Adoption*, paper presented at the Fifth Biennial National Conference of the National Association for Loss and Grief, Australia, 1987

Verrier, Nancy Newton. *The Primal Wound: Understanding the Adopted Child*, Gateway Press, Inc, USA, 1993

The Invisible Men of Adoption

Verrier, Nancy Newton. *Coming Home to Self*, Gateway Press, Inc, USA, 2003

Victorian Government Department of Human Services. *Adoption: Myth and Reality – The Adoption and Family Records Service in Victoria*, Australia, 2009

Watkins Jenny and Reynolds, Robert. *A Work in Progress*, 'Proceedings of 7th Australian Adoption Conference', Hobart, 2000, pp367–376

Wells, Sue. *Within Me, Without Me Adoption: an open and shut case?*, Scarlet Press, United Kingdom, 1994

Winkler, Robin and van Keppel, Margaret. *Relinquishing Mothers in Adoption: Their Long-term Adjustment*, Melbourne Institute of Family Studies, Monograph No. 3, Australia, 1984

Witney, Celia. *The experiences of unmarried fathers whose children were surrendered for adoption: some conclusions and comments*, 'NPN Newsletter' No 33, April 2003, p12

Wood, Randy. *A Birthfather Reflects on the Reunion Process*, 'CUB Communicator', Fall 2002, p8

Woolmington, Nicola. *Searching*, M&A Film Productions Pty Limited and Australian Film Finance Corporation Pty Limited, Australia, 1992

*****

Personal note: I told the bulk of my adoption story in the first section of ***Ever After: Fathers and the Impact of Adoption*** (2004). In 2009, I was reunited with my son, Mark. Previously, Kay (Mark's birth mother) and I had achieved a rapprochement.

*****

"*By endurance we conquer.*" – The family motto of Ernest Shackleton

www.ingramcontent.com/pod-product-compliance
Lightning Source LLC
Chambersburg PA
CBHW070738160426
43192CB00009B/1487